JOHN HARE

Why Bother Being Good?

The Place of God in the Moral Life

WIPF & STOCK · Eugene, Oregon

Wipf and Stock Publishers
199 W 8th Ave, Suite 3
Eugene, OR 97401

Why Bother Being Good?
The Place of God in the Moral Life
By Hare, John E.
Copyright©2002 by Hare, John E.
ISBN 13: 978-1-61097-050-1
Publication date 10/11/2010
Previously published by InterVarsity Press US, 2002

Originally published by InterVarsity Press as
Why Bother Being Good? by John Hare.
© 2002 by John Hare. Published by
permission of InterVarsity Press,
P.O. Box 1400, Downers Grove, IL 60515, USA.

Contents

Introduction

Why we should bother being good is the main topic of this book. The last six chapters of the book are about why we *should* be morally good, or where the authority of morality comes from. But this question does not arise unless morality is "doable," and we *can* be morally good. This is the topic of the first four chapters of the book. I cover it first because we need to see that we can be good before it is worth asking why we should be. The argument of the book as a whole is that the morality we are familiar with has roots in the Christian faith, and it starts to break down when its Christian context is removed. In particular, we lose a clear sense of how we can meet the moral demand and what its source of authority is.

In chapter one I discuss what being morally good means, and I raise the problem of the moral gap. Morality, I say, is a set of norms for how we should live, and the norms exist to support or express values we hold dear. The norms are organized by a central directive that constrains the actions we are morally permitted to do and the sorts of people we are morally permitted to be. I claim that the moral demand is too high for us given the natural human capacities we are born with. This is what creates the problem of the moral gap. How *can* we be morally good? According to Christian doctrine, God first calls us to live a certain way and then offers us various kinds of assis-

tance to live that way. If we no longer believe in God's assistance,
how can we reasonably be held to the same demand?

In chapter two I look at various alternatives to God's assistance
proposed by contemporary thinkers. All of these alternatives seem to
me to fail and so to leave us in the moral gap. In chapter three I discuss three Christian doctrines—atonement, justification and sanctification—that describe how God's assistance is supposed to work
inside us. Then in chapter four I look at the doctrine of providence
and what it says about the kind of assistance in the world outside of
us God gives us for the moral life. We need to believe that the world
makes some kind of moral sense.

In the second part of the book the question is why we *should* try
to be morally good. What is the source of the authority of morality?
According to Christian doctrine the source is God's will and call. In
chapter five I mention some alternatives to this view. As in the first
part of the book, I proceed by looking at non-Christian answers to
the question to see if they are sufficient. One alternative is that the
authority of morality is just as obvious as the authority of sense perception, and it does not have a source at all. A second alternative is
that the authority comes from human nature, and we have to live
morally in order to be completely human. Another possibility is that
reason demands we be moral, and it would be irrational to refuse
such a demand. Finally, we may be required to be moral because we
are members of a community that demands it as a condition of our
being true to our social identity. In all four of these alternatives we
get a way to preserve the authority of morality without appealing to
God. In chapters six to nine I look at each of these alternatives in
turn, trying to discern what is right with each claim but concluding
that each one is insufficient. In the final chapter I discuss the notion
of autonomy. How can we be autonomous if we are living under the
authority of God's call?

The book is a retrieval project. It tries to retrieve from traditional Christian doctrine an understanding of how we can be morally good and why we should be so. There is a third part of this retrieval project for moral theory which does not appear in this book. I do not try to say much about how to live a good life. I do not discuss the place of moral rules as opposed to the judgment of particular cases. I have not tried to describe the structure of a good life or how it is shaped by an overall life story. I have not pursued the topic of how to receive guidance or hear the call of God. The first part of the book relates primarily to the doctrine of Christ's work and the second part to the doctrine of God the Father. The third part (which I have not yet written) relates primarily to the doctrine of the Holy Spirit.

If all the arguments in this book work, what I have shown is that the morality we are familiar with requires a theological background if it is going to make sense. This does not prove the theological doctrines true. There is always the alternative possibility of rejecting morality as we are familiar with it. All I have shown is that if we want to hang on to this morality and reject the theology, then we will have to find some substitute to do the work that the theology used to do. It is not going to be easy to find such a substitute.

This book is the first in a series that will be written by professors at Calvin College who have been appointed Calvin Lecturer for a year. The program takes the lecturer to a number of campuses in Canada, the United States and Europe, where he or she gives a general public lecture as well as more specialized lectures to particular departments and groups on campus. The academic discipline will be different each year. In my case it is the discipline of philosophy, and within this the subdiscipline of ethics. The topic of my general public lecture was "Does Morality Need God?"

One of the goals of this series is that it should address an audience beyond the specialization of each writer. This is a great privilege. How many professional philosophers get a chance to write for a nonspecialized audience rather than for the small group of other professional philosophers within the guild? I have tried to be faithful to this goal, and I have accordingly observed two constraints on my usual style of writing. First, I have allowed myself no footnotes, though I have included a bibliography for each chapter at the end of the book. My work is usually festooned with footnotes because I tend to make a lot of small qualifications and because I feel accountable to the discipline; I do not like using ideas without making reference to the places where I first encountered them. I have persuaded myself not to worry about this here because the curious reader can usually find more detailed references in the scholarly work I have written earlier. In particular, the references in the first four chapters of this book can be found in *The Moral Gap (MG):* chapter one in *MG* chapter one; chapter two in *MG* chapters four, five and seven; chapter three in *MG* chapters eight and ten; chapter four in *MG* chapter three. The references in the last six chapters of this book can mostly be found in *God's Call (GC):* chapter six in *GC* chapter one (and *MG* chapter five); chapter seven in *GC* chapter two; chapters eight and nine in *MG* chapter six; and chapter ten in *GC* chapter three.

The second constraint I have observed is that I have allowed myself no philosophical jargon. For example, I have excluded all words ending with "ism," unless they are in general use. So "relativism" is allowed, but "prescriptivism" is not. This constraint has been less taxing than I thought it was going to be. I have discovered that most technical terms can be deleted in favor of ordinary English if the author tries hard enough, and I think the result has in fact been an improvement in clarity.

I have kept in, however, some ideas that are quite challenging. I am not apologizing for this. I think the ideas are worth working through, and I hope my readers will agree after they have read the book. It is an exciting time to be a moral philosopher and a Christian. There are many ideas from the recent history of the discipline that can be helpful in understanding the faith, and many doctrines of the faith that can be helpful in making sense of the discipline in its present state. But the connections in both directions are complex, and it takes sustained intellectual work to understand them.

One way I have tried to make this book interesting to more than just philosophers is to put in nonphilosophical material like poetry and a number of fictional examples from a connected narrative about a family whose mother (Rosa) is the central character. This is risky for someone who is not an expert in poetry or narrative. I ask the reader to excuse any crudeness and naiveté in these attempts. The fictional examples are not intended to make up a good story on its own merits. They are servants to the philosophy, and I have restrained them from growing beyond that role. The interpretation of the poetry also has a primarily philosophical motivation, and I have resisted the urge to go more deeply into the meaning of each poem.

I hope that people who are not philosophers and also people who are not Christians will read this book. Christians who are not philosophers will find in the book some new and I hope useful ways to think about their faith. Thinking philosophically has the power to bring a fresh understanding of the tradition, and it connects this tradition with developments in contemporary thought. Philosophers and others who are not Christians will find a way to think about ethics that connects directly to many of the great philosophical texts of the last two thousand years. They will benefit from the book not only by better understanding their own tradition but also by finding resources in Christianity for dealing with some serious difficulties in contemporary ethical theory.

I want to be forthcoming about my own ecclesiastical and philosophical background. My church background is Anglican, especially its broadly Calvinist wing. I have not aimed to write from a narrow Anglo-Calvinist perspective, but undoubtedly my background has colored how I see Christianity and its relation to moral life. I have tried to read widely in other Christian traditions, and I hope that what I say will be useful to people who do not come from this particular part of the worldwide church. My philosophical training has been in the analytic tradition, specializing (both in undergraduate and graduate work) in ancient Greek philosophy. Again, this has certainly shaped how I see and do philosophy, but I have tried to read widely outside this tradition, and I hope the book will not be narrow in its assumptions about method and practice. Apart from the Greeks, the main philosophical influences on this book have been Duns Scotus, Immanuel Kant and the ordinary language school of twentieth-century philosophy.

I am grateful to many people who have helped me with this project. I received good advice on many of the campuses I visited during the lectureship. My colleagues in the Calvin philosophy department have read through much of the material with me in one form or another, and the book is much better as a result. My friends in the Thursday Morning Group showed me that there is reassuring common ground between professional philosophers who are Christians and the educated Christian public. C. Stephen Evans, James Ingram, Cornelius Plantinga Jr., William Jensen, Samuel Jolman, Benjamin Lipscomb and Terence Cuneo read the manuscript and gave me useful criticisms. To all these people, and others I have not mentioned here who have helped me, many thanks.

1

Morality

In this book I am going to ask what morality has to do with God. What is morality? It has two components: it contains a set of norms for social practice, and it organizes these under a central directive. Examples of moral norms are that we should keep our promises, we should not commit murder, we should be grateful to people who are kind to us, and we should not nurse grudges. Some of these norms tell us what to do, and some of them tell us what not to do. Some are norms for action, and some are for character or attitude. Some of them are also legal norms, but some of them are not. They are all, however, norms for social practice in the sense that they are taught within a society, and they are the glue that holds a society together. Parents try to teach morality to their children, and the members of a society maintain the norms by what they expect of each other. All these norms respond to values that we perceive, and that the norms exist to support or express. For example, the norm that tells us not to commit murder responds to the value of human life. The norm that tells us not to nurse grudges responds to the values of relationship and reconciliation. These norms, and the values behind them, can compete with each other, in the sense that we sometimes have to choose between them.

To help with these choices, morality has a second component: an organizing directive. It tells us to take the largest available perspective on the world and from this perspective to care about the well-being of everybody, and to respect the unique and equal value of each person. In section three we will discuss this definition phrase by phrase. The rough idea is that our norms are organized around the ideal of a global but also a fully detailed concern for every person.

The background within Christianity to the first component (the norms and the values they respond to) is the commandments of the law, especially the second group of the Ten Commandments given to Moses on Mt. Sinai (Ex 20:12-17). Jesus also gave us the Sermon on the Mount (Mt 5—7), and the epistles are full of counsel and advice about how to treat each other. For example, "But now you must rid yourselves of all such things as these: anger, rage, malice, slander, and abusive language from your lips. Do not lie to each other, since you have taken off your old self with its practices and have put on the new self, which is being renewed in knowledge in the image of its Creator" (Col 3:8-10, translation altered by the author). The background to the second component (the organizing directive) is the second of the great commandments Jesus gives, to love the neighbor as the self (Mt 22:39-40; see also Lev 19:18).

These various commandments within Christianity are the background for the two components of morality as we are familiar with it. This is not to say that all Christians over the surface of the globe and all Christians over the history of the church have been familiar with the set of norms and values "we" are now familiar with, or that they have all had the organizing directive stated above. Section five in this chapter says more about what I mean by "we." Nor am I claiming that Christianity is the only background for morality as "we" are familiar with it. Chapter seven discusses how we still feel the power of values that were articulated in ancient Greece and are inconsistent with Christianity.

My claim in this book is that the commandments about our relation to our neighbor belong together with the commandments about our relation to God. To put this another way, the two groups of the Ten Commandments given on Sinai belong together as a single unit, as do the two great commandments that Jesus gave us. Loving our neighbor belongs in the context of loving God. If we try to separate neighbor-love from God-love, we will be left with various kinds of incoherence. This book will concentrate on two problems: whether we can keep the neighbor-commandments, and why we should try to keep them. So the project of the book is in part a kind of retrieval. I want to go back and recapture the theological background against which morality as we are familiar with it makes sense. But the project is not merely retrieval or merely nostalgic. I am not saying we need to go back, for instance, to the middle ages. What we have discovered about morality in the modern period, when it is coordinated with this background, is valuable and worth preserving.

After discussing the two components of morality, the chapter will examine the relation between value and obligation, or between "good" and "right." I will then explain what I mean by "we" and "our." The final section will examine what I call "the moral gap" between the moral demand and our natural capacities, and I will briefly mention some strategies for dealing with this gap used by those who do not believe in God and those who do. (Chapters two and three will further explore these strategies.)

Norms and Values

What is a norm? I do not mean the purely statistical sense of the word. A statistical norm would be, "Humans consume two thousand calories a day." If a biologist says this, she is not thereby recommending this level of intake. She is simply reporting that this is the number of calories that humans (as opposed to, say, armadillos) normally consume. The statistical fact disguises a huge variety in the actual caloric intakes of different human beings. In the sense in which norms are a component of morality, however, they are not merely facts about how we live, but they tell us how we *should* live. The norms respond to values, which they exist to support or express. For example, the norm that tells us not to lie responds to the value of truth and truthfulness. We can describe the values endorsed by a society by giving a profile of what its members tend to love and hate. The same is true of an individual. Here is one example.

Rosa loves truthfulness; she feels uneasy whenever she is put in a situation that calls for less than the full truth. She loves her husband and her children and is faithful to them even at significant cost to herself, even though she is also willing to tell them the truth about their faults when she thinks this is necessary and not cruel. She loves meeting new people but hates it when they are in need and she cannot do anything to help them. This means that she is constantly juggling her time because there is a bottomless pit of people with needs to be met. She hates injustice, especially where it creates barriers between people of race or class, and she goes out of her way to break these barriers down by personal contact. She loves playing and listening to good music and therefore practices hard when the piece is challenging and she cannot yet play it to her satisfaction. Especially she loves chamber music because it combines her delight in music with her talent for friendship. She hates sloppy and out-of-tune playing, and she hates the style of putting little scoops and slides into classical music to pander to sentimental taste. She loves a good joke and hearty laughter, as long as it is not hurting someone else. Often the situations she finds funniest are those where her own pretensions have been exposed. She has, finally, an instinctive courtesy that puts other people at their ease with her, and she loves to establish immediate contact at a personal level with a waitress, for example, or the salesperson at a department store.

If I judge that Rosa is a good person, I am endorsing her perceived values. I am claiming that this profile of what she loves and hates describes a magnetic pull toward what is actually good and a repulsion from what is actually bad. Rosa's character will be coherent to the extent that the values that pull her can be achieved together. If they are themselves in conflict, or in conflict because of her situation, then she will tend to be pulled apart. Sometimes even good people, or especially such people, are divided in this way. I have deliberately constructed the profile so that it mixes norms of different kinds: moral and aesthetic, standards of humor and of etiquette. These are hard to separate out from each other in Rosa's case.

What makes moral norms *moral*? It is relatively easy to say what morality is not. In some societies it is rude to touch your food with your hands when you eat, and in other societies it is expected. For example, I recently visited a village called Njola in southern Zambia, where my daughter was working. There we were given a bowl of thick maize-porridge (called "nshima") and another bowl of vegetable or meat relish, and we were told to form the nshima into a kind of spoon with our hands, and use it to dip into the relish. This is a rule of etiquette, not morality. When we look at a Cézanne painting of apples arranged on a table and admire the sense of solidity and structure, we are using aesthetic, not moral, standards to judge the painting. But there can be overlap. For example, morality is not defined in terms of art or beauty, but it is morally wrong to burn Cézanne's paintings. Similarly with standards of humor, we can judge that a story was boring, though morality had nothing to do with it; but it is morally doubtful whether we should laugh at Holocaust jokes. In general, we can say that morality is not defined in terms of art, or etiquette, or humor. But what can we say that morality is, in contrast with the other kinds of norms?

The word *moral* comes to us from the Latin *mos*, which means "custom" or "habit." The word *ethical* comes from the Greek *ethos*, again meaning "habit" or "character" or "custom." But to know what habits and what social practices a speaker is referring to by saying "moral" or "ethical," we have to know the cultural context of the speaker. My claim is that the norms for character and life we now identify as moral are organized around the directive that tells us to take the largest available perspective on the world, and from that perspective to care about the well-being of everybody, and to respect the unique and equal value of each person. Adopting this account of morality helps us distinguish moral norms from the other kinds of norms that I have mentioned, for art and etiquette and humor.

These other norms respond to values that have their own roughly independent domains, such as beauty or social convention or what is funny. I say "independent" because a work of art can be cruel and still be aesthetically satisfying (like some of the paintings of Francis Bacon). A social convention can be cruel, but conforming to it can still be required of a gentleman or a lady (like dueling in Europe, or binding women's feet in China). Cruel jokes can still be funny; indeed they often are. Despite this independence, there is overlap with morality. Beauty contributes to our well-being, and that is why it is morally wrong to burn the paintings; however, some successful works of art can be created and used for evil purposes. Social conventions are morally necessary, because our happiness requires some kind of roughly predictable order in our relations; but also some conventions are morally harmful. A good sense of humor is morally valuable, an important part of our flourishing as human beings; but also we feel, or should feel, morally constrained in the jokes we tell and laugh at.

In short, a norm tells us how we should live, and it responds to a value, which it exists to support or express. (Chapter six further explores the objective reality of value.) A moral norm is one that is organized around the central directive of a global but fully detailed concern for the well-being of every person.

The Organizing Directive

The organizing directive has three parts: (1) It tells us to try to think from the position of a person who can assess and who cares most about the well-being of the whole. (2) It tells us to count persons as the most valuable things in the world and to treat them as having equal value with each other. (3) It tells us to value the uniqueness of persons as much as what they have in common.

First, we do not endorse every impulse that we have. The organizing directive gives us a screen. We have the ideal of judging the situation and our response from a position that can assess and that cares most about the well-being of the whole. What is "the whole" here? Suppose Rosa is feeling the pull toward helping someone she meets, and she is trying to judge whether to endorse this sense of pull. She can ask whether making this choice is consistent with all the things she cares about. That is a kind of personal whole. But she can go beyond this. She can ask whether it is consistent with what is good for her family, her friends, her associates and fellow-citizens, or all the people (wherever they live) who would be affected by the way she lives her life. Here she will reach something like the whole of humanity.

But reflection does not need to stop here. Her life also affects animals and the whole earth in which animals and people live together. She can ask whether her choice is consistent with what is good for the whole thing. I am not trying to lay out a complete ethical theory here, and so I will not try to be more specific. I will not try to analyze "good" in terms of interests, or natural ends, or rational preferences, or to say whether plants are included, or mountains, or other planets. My point is just that we screen morally by stepping back-

ward, as it were—by asking more and more inclusively whether what
we are proposing to do fits the well-being and integrity of the whole
of which we are a part.

A believer in God will think that when I say, "from a position that
can assess and that cares most about the well-being of the whole," I
mean, "from the position of God." It is God, after all, who can see
the whole. Chapter eight looks at whether belief in God is required
for a good account of the position which the organizing directive
requires. For now, assume that a human being, an ideal observer,
could see and care about the whole of which she is a part. Her pre-
scriptions for our situations could then be a standard for what is good
and what is right in those situations. It is clear that we do not in fact
occupy this position, even though we may try to approximate it in
our moral judgments. We are prevented not merely by the fact that
our knowledge is finite, but by the fact that we seem to have an in-
built preference for our own well-being that is inconsistent with caring most about the whole.

This position that sees and cares about the whole does not by itself
give us morality. The ideal observer might proceed in different ways
from this viewpoint. Suppose she thinks that cockroaches are the
most valuable creatures on earth, and everything should be done to
make them prosper, even at the cost of great self-sacrifice. She might
smuggle them into all her friends' houses and into shops and
churches to help them take their proper dominant place in the world.
However, the moral point of view requires that she count *persons* as
the most valuable things in the world, and that she treat them as having equal value with each other. This is the second part of the organizing directive. The morally ideal observer's frame of mind is not
merely impartial. Contempt and hatred can be impartial as much as
love. It is possible to hate all human beings equally, including oneself.
But the morally ideal observer has to be impartially benevolent, caring more for people's well-being than for anything else and valuing

equally the well-being of them all.

Rosa loves to establish immediate contact at a personal level with the waitress who is serving her. She does not treat her merely as a conveyer-belt on legs, to get the food from the kitchen to her table as quickly as possible. How does she show that she respects her server as a person equal in value to herself? She takes seriously what the waitress herself wants and makes those ends her own ends as far as she can in that context. Rosa may have had a long, hard day; however, she recognizes that the waitress may well have had a long day too, and impatience makes everything worse for both of them. The two of them are worth the same.

Whether the morally ideal observer extends such moral concern beyond persons (or whether such an observer might count, for example, cockroaches as persons) is a question I will not deal with here. My sense is that our morality is changing, and that we are beginning to count morality as extending beyond our relations to other people (but not as far as cockroaches). I think this extension is right. But even so, as long as we grant that humans are higher in value than other animals (which deep ecologists tend to deny), human well-being will be valued more.

Thus the screening by the organizing directive is, first, an attempt to think from the position of a person who can assess and who cares most about the well-being of the whole, and, second, it counts persons as the most valuable things in the world and treats them as having equal value with each other. The third component is not as much part of the consensus about our morality as points one and two. I already stressed the sameness of human persons as counting the same morally just because of being persons. I did not ask what it is about human persons that makes them the most valuable thing in the world. It is tempting to answer that, whatever it is, it must be something they have in common, like humanity itself.

However, there is one strand in the tradition we belong to that denies this. This is the third point. It holds that what distinguishes us humans from each other is more valuable than, or at least equally valuable with, what we have in common. The idea is that we each have, as persons, an individual essence, which is unique to us. The background in the Christian Bible is that God gives to each person in heaven a name written on a white stone, and although God knows this name, we do not yet know it (Rev 2:17). This name (like ancient Hebrew names in general) tells what kind the named thing is. This is like Jesus giving "Peter" (*petros,* meaning rock) as a name to Simon. On this view, then, treating a person as a person is as much a respect for difference as it is a recognition of sameness. Because persons are the sorts of things they are, respecting them is both recognizing the sameness and respecting the difference. Respect honors what we do not know about someone just as much as what we know.

Attraction and Constraint

What is the relation between the two components of morality, namely the different norms with the values they respond to and the organizing directive for those norms? The values attract us like a magnet. But it is also true that the norms and the organizing directive involve a large measure of constraint. The family of terms that belong here clusters around "right," our moral obligation and duty, rather than "good," what we are drawn to and what we love. Obligation can tell us both what to do and what not to do, but it often operates in situations where there is a contrary attraction or inclination that has to be restrained.

Rosa is a teacher. She is taking a nap after getting back from school, and she is faced with the obligation to get up and prepare for the next day's class project. She is finally awakened by a telephone call from her parents about Christmas plans. She feels like telling a little fib about a prior commitment and is faced with the obligation not to lie.

Obligations can come from roles we adopt (like the role of teacher) or roles we do not choose (like the role of being someone's child) or just from being people, not in any particular role at all. In all these cases obligations can have the feel of burden and weight. As Ogden Nash puts it:

O Duty,
Why hast thou not the visage of a sweetie or a cutie?
Why displayest thou the countenance of the kind of conscientious
  organizing spinster
That the minute you see her you are aginster?
Why glitter thy spectacles so ominously?
Why art thou clad so abominously?
Why art thou so different from Venus?
And why do thou and I have so few interests mutually in common
  between us?

This sense of burden comes from focusing on cases where duty and inclination have come apart. But the ideal case is where they coincide. The best kind of person likes doing what she is also under an obligation to do. The theological doctrine of sanctification gives an account of progress toward this happy condition, and there are nontheological accounts of moral development that do the same. Rather than thinking of obligation and duty in terms of burden, it is better to think of them as a screening procedure that gives permission for us to act or be a certain way. The notion of permission is central here. "It is my duty" does not mean "I am (morally) permitted"; duty is required and not merely permitted. But the person with a healthy sense of duty is constantly checking for permission, as a good driver checks in the rear-view mirror.

The moral agent wants to check whether what she is doing fits the good of the whole, seen in terms of the equal and unique value of each person. If it fits, she may do it, and this kind of permission is an affirmation, not a denial. In a similar way a composer checks each new phrase in his piece against his sense of the whole composition, and experiences this sense of the whole as liberating, since it gives him boundaries within which his creativity can flourish. It gives his piece a good shape to grow into. From the notion of permission we can derive the notion of what we are *not* permitted to do or be (we are prohibited) and the notion of what we are *not* permitted *not* to do or be (we are required). Rosa is prohibited from lying in order to escape, and she is required to get up and prepare her materials for class. Since she is drawn toward truthfulness and toward teaching well, her inclination and her sense of permission will coincide here. But this does not mean that telling the truth and doing her work stop being her duty. It just means that she has a welcome sense of fit.

The sense of duty is not a second-best motivation for virtuous action. We are tempted to think that the best kind of person helps others not out of duty but out of a direct interest in their welfare. If I ask my students, "Would you rather be visited in the hospital by someone who loves you or by someone who is visiting out of duty?" it is obvious what they will say. But the question assumes the kind of separation between inclination and the sense of duty that Ogden Nash assumes, and which I have said is not the best case of duty. The best kind of person visits both because she should and because she wants to, and she does not feel any tension between the two. In the same way Rosa practices her instrument because she should (the piece needs it) and because she wants to. The fact that she wants to practice doesn't stop the practice being needed. But certainly many of us are not good in this kind of way. We do feel a separation between duty and inclination. And we can even describe a "pathological" sense of duty in which there is no inclination, no attraction at all, but only the grim sense of constraint. This may be the clearest case where the sense of duty can be seen in isolation, all by itself. However, this does not mean that it is the best sense of duty for a person to have.

Putting the matter this way, we can see that attraction and constraint both play central roles in morality, but different roles. If we understand "right" roughly in terms of constraint and "good" in terms of attraction, there will be different kinds of priority between them. The right is not the source of the good (not prior in that sense). The good is like a magnet, with its own power of attraction. But the right has veto power, priority in this different sense. This is not an alien authority that it has over the good. Rather, the right is the fittingness of some particular good with the good of the whole, seen in terms of the equal and unique value of each person.

Normative and Descriptive

A central group of norms exists in all the cultures we know about. For example, the moral institution of promise-making (or at least something very like promising) and some notion of wrongful killing exist in all societies. Cultural anthropologists have provided a list of "human universals" that number in the hundreds. But if we look at the different societies across the earth and across the earth's history, they show both this similarity and a large variety in the norms by which they live.

The variety can be seen by comparing central scenes from four epics, written at intervals of about eight centuries. In Homer's *Iliad* Achilles, who has been sulking in his tent, finally decides to fight again, for the sake of his comrades, but mostly to avenge the death of his dear friend at the hands of Hector. Compare Aeneas in Virgil's *Aeneid*, who is modeled on Achilles, but who relates to his passions very differently. He visits Carthage and falls in love with its queen, Dido, and then the gods summon him on to his destiny, which is to found the city of Rome. "Italy must be my love and my homeland now," he says to the distraught queen, and then he sails away. The Homeric heroes have no country like the one Virgil is celebrating, and so they have no sense of duty like this. They have loyalty to each other, but not to something like "the destiny of Rome."

If we compare Aeneas with Beowulf (eight centuries later), we again sense different norms in play. For example, nothing in Homer or Virgil is like Beowulf's central encounter with the evil spirit-monster Grendel, descended from Cain. The earlier epics do not describe that kind of demonic evil, in part because *Beowulf* was influenced by contact with Christianity. There is no sense in Homer's *Iliad* of a cosmic struggle between good and evil, only of the struggle of some divine beings with others, in which humans are then implicated. In Virgil, to the extent that there is a cosmic struggle, it is seen through the lens of politics or the destiny of Rome. Finally, Milton's *Paradise Lost*, which comes another eight hundred years after *Beowulf*, is a different world again. Nothing in the earlier epics is like the focal scene of Adam choosing to eat the apple so that Eve will not be alone in her sin, making conjugal companionship more important than the risk of losing his own salvation. He will not take a different partner, even one grown from another of his ribs, and he puts this personal relationship ahead of his relationship with his Creator.

Yet despite all these differences, we also sense kinship. These works are all recognizably epics, and they all have heroes facing crisis, showing excellence of character, being tempted to defect from their appointed role, feeling anger and love and sorrow and shame. We could not be moved by their plight or admire their tenacity if we did not feel this kinship with them. So there is both radical difference and significant overlap. This is true not just historically but geographically. It is possible to move from Grand Rapids, Michigan, to southern Zambia and feel this same mixture of disorientation and basic familiarity.

Thus the same set of norms is not present in all cultures or societies, and neither is the organizing directive. For much of human history people have felt a sense of obligation to others in the same tribe or nation, but not to other human beings as such. Societies that do not have this idea of equal human standing have moralities that are different from ours to a greater or lesser extent.

However, we need to make a distinction between descriptive and normative accounts of the nature of morality. There are two ways of asking and answering the question, What is morality? We might be asking, How should we live? and the answer will be that we should keep our promises, be grateful to our benefactors, and so on. This is a normative account. But we might also be asking, about some particular societies or about societies in general, what their moralities are in fact like. The answer might be that in societies XYZ they value kinds of life ABC. To say this is not to endorse such an evaluation as directing how we or they should live life. It is merely a descriptive account of the practices in XYZ. In the same way, the biologist's report, "Humans eat two thousand calories a day," is just a report and not yet an endorsement. The second section of this chapter claimed that we count norms as moral if they are organized around a certain directive. Is this suggestion about the organizing directive normative or descriptive? It is both. We should organize our moral norms around this principle. But the suggestion is also an answer to a descriptive question about one particular society, namely, our own. The question is, What norms do we in our society call moral norms? The answer is, Those organized around this directive.

The terms *we* and *our* are often both descriptive and normative, because there are normative criteria hiding behind the inclusion or exclusion of a person from "our" group. Thus the British upper classes used to have a code, "NQOCD," which meant "not quite our class, dear," and was used when it was embarrassing to be more openly contemptuous. They determined who was in "our class" and who was out by an elaborate set of normative terms like *gentleman*. When I ask, What do we in our society call moral? who are the "we"? Is the term descriptive or normative or both? I mean it to be descriptive, to include the people living in the places I have lived in

North America and Europe, and many other places in the world that are like these. My claim is that there is much common ground in the conceptions of morality to be found in this expanding culture (as well as much common failure to live by these standards). If someone lives in these places and does not accept the idea of human equality, for example, he or she will be at odds with the dominant culture but will still belong to the "we." This means that "we" have many different norms that we live by, as well as much common ground. Any workable political system for these parts of the world has to acknowledge both the variety and the broad (though not universal) consensus.

The implication of the central claims of this book is that many of "us" do not have the background beliefs that (if I am right) make sense of the norms we endorse. This itself is a normative and perhaps presumptuous claim, since "make sense" is a normative concept. Coherence or making sense is a *virtue* of structures of thought (though not their only virtue). If I am right about this lack of coherence, it is important that those of us who do believe in this background be allowed to articulate in the public arena this connection of norm and background. For if morality does not make sense without the background, then when the background is rejected, morality will start to break down in various ways; that breakdown is harmful to people whether they believe in the background or not.

The Moral Gap

We need "right" in addition to "good" because we are finite and because we are self-interested. We do not see the good of the whole, and even where we do see that the good of other people is at stake, we tend to prefer our own good. I am not saying that there is something wrong with aiming at our own good. But the key moral question is how we rank the preferences. As we look at our individual situations, something can seem bad for us individually and good for the whole. Do we put our own good first and the good of the whole second, so that we will only do what is good for everybody (and everything) as a whole if we can see that it is good for us? Or do we reverse this priority, and put the good of the whole first, so that we will only do what suits us if we can see that it fits the good of the whole? I think we are born with the tendency to be drawn more toward our own good (the first of these rankings). So in order to be morally good people we need the constraint of the notion of "right" to screen our pursuits. But even if we did not have such a natural tendency, we would still need the "right." Because we are finite, we feel the magnetic pull of the good in a very fragmentary and incomplete way. We need some kind of procedure for checking at least provisionally whether the good we feel drawn to is consistent with the flourishing of everyone (and everything) as a whole.

We have here the structure of the moral gap. There is, first, the moral demand, which combines the good and the right in the way I have been suggesting. It brings our lives under the organizing directive. But this demand is too high for us given our natural capacities, the capacities we are born with. These capacities are the second part of the structure.

Here is an example to make this vivid. In Zambia the per capita income is just over a dollar a day. There are many people there, especially children (and especially AIDS orphans), who starve to death each year. When I go to a movie in America, which costs about seven dollars, I am spending money that could keep a child alive in Zambia for a week. If I look at this from the perspective of the good of the whole, counting each human being as having equal and unique value, how can I justify this expense?

Perhaps it is an important movie, full of beauty and truth. But then maybe it is *Rocky V.* Perhaps I need to see the movie in order to do my job and be an informed critic of the culture. But perhaps *Rocky I* through *IV* were enough for that purpose. Maybe I am in danger of burning out if I do not get some relaxation and recreation. But why not go for a walk in the park instead? Maybe this is a good chance to have some time with my children, and I justify spending more on my family because I have been given special charge of them. But is this movie really the best way to have quality time with my family?

I think when all this has been said, we will still be left with the sense that morality requires a significantly lower standard of living than most of us in the West currently enjoy. This question of how I spend my resources is a tormenting one; it can lead to self-hatred and hatred of the whole North American way of life. It is not just the movie, but the CD player, the new couch, the down jacket. The question can also lead to despair because the extent of the need is so great and my resources are pitifully small. We will return to this in chapter two. (I have discussed it also in chapter seven of *Ethics and International Affairs.*) For now, the point is that the ethical demand is too high for us given our natural capacities. How can we live by it?

Very often people add a third item to this structure of a gap between the demand and our capacities. They imagine a being or beings who do not have our limitations and who are the source of the demand. Earlier I put this in terms of an ideal observer. We imagine morality as what someone would demand from us who was not finite in knowledge and was not self-interested in the way we are. It is interesting that this feature of our morality has survived into the modern age even among theorists who no longer believe in the God who was the original "ideal observer" in the tradition. They do not suppose that the ideal observer actually has to exist. But they seem to be drawn to thinking of morality as if such a being or beings did exist.

This structure of three parts is not only found in societies influenced by Judaism, Christianity and Islam. Aristotle tells us that the best life would be superior to the human level, but we ought not to follow the proverb writers and "think human, since you are human," or "think mortal, since you are mortal"; rather, as far as we can, we ought to be immortal (i.e., like the immortal gods). I taught for a week in China, and I was introduced there to the thought of Chu Hsi (from the twelfth century) and visited the monastery where he taught. He says that we should think of human beings (at least most of them) as prevented from a clear view of right principle (of which heaven is the source) because they are like pearls lying in muddy water.

However, the structure of the moral gap has an internal problem. It seems unreasonable, indeed incoherent, to hold people accountable to standards that they are unable to reach. One way to put this is that "ought" implies "can." This is true if we understand it to mean that if a person cannot do something, the question whether she ought to do it does not arise. If the moral demand is too high for us, the question whether we ought to live by it does not arise.

Rosa once took her son Ned, when he was a baby, to visit her pastor. The pastor asked to hold him, and Rosa handed him over a bit reluctantly. She had just fed him and she knew that he was likely to spit up. The pastor held him against his chest, patted him soothingly, and Ned promptly vomited on his shirt. Rosa was mortified, but she did not blame Ned. He was not in control of his digestion, and there was no sense in her saying that he ought to have been. A cardinal principle of her child-raising has always been that she should only hold her children accountable to standards they were able to meet.

Christianity has a particular take on the moral gap. It holds that the third item in the structure of the moral gap is God. God intervenes to change the second part of the structure (our natural capacities) so that they become adequate to the first part of the structure (the moral demand).

The prestige of this view has declined in elite Western culture. The result is a series of attempts to deal with the problem of the moral gap without bringing in God's assistance. There are three main strategies. We will look at an example of each one now and then expand on each idea in the next chapter. The first strategy is to keep the demand where it is and pretend that we have the capacity by our own devices to live by it. For example, we pretend that it is only ignorance and lack of education that stops us from being moral, not a fundamental failure of the will. The second strategy is to acknowledge the limits to the capacities we are born with and naturally develop, and then to lower the demand to fit them. For example, we claim that we are not naturally suited to impartial benevolence, and therefore we do not have obligations to starving children in Africa we do not know. The third strategy is to keep the demand and the capacities where they are on the traditional picture of the moral gap, and then try to find an alternative to God's assistance in bridging the gap. For example, we claim there is some life force within the universe that naturally emerges into higher and higher forms of consciousness until it reaches moral maturity. If these three strategies fail, as I think they do, we are left in the moral gap.

I am not arguing here, or anywhere in the book, that only believers in God can be morally good. There are no doubt many nonbelievers whose moral lives put many believers to shame. However, I think there is a kind of incoherence in their lives, since I believe God is the enabler of the morally good life and the source of the authority of morality. There is nothing particularly surprising in such incoherence. We take our beliefs from so many different sources that a totally coherent set of beliefs is likely to be the exception rather than the rule. Consider, for example, the different beliefs about the world we take from our fathers and mothers, and how these beliefs sit next to each other in our minds, compromising with each other rather like our parents themselves. Incoherence in a set of beliefs is common, but that does not excuse it. Our reason still gives us the task of aiming at coherence. Incoherence in our beliefs about morality has consequences. The moral lives of religious believers and nonbelievers are likely to be different, and we will look at this in the final chapter.

What are the resources for bridging the gap that Christianity provides? This is the topic of chapter three, which discusses the doctrines of atonement, justification and sanctification. Christ dies for our sins, God imputes to us Christ's righteousness, and the Holy Spirit comes to dwell in us to lead us to holiness. These doctrines concern primarily the problem *inside* ourselves. But there are also problems about what kind of world *outside* ourselves we should believe we are born into, given that we have to sustain the moral life. We have to believe that the world makes some kind of moral sense, even in the midst of our experience of tragedy and evil. This is the topic of chapter four, which discusses the resources provided by the Christian doctrine of providence.

2

The Moral Gap
Without God

If we do not bring in God's assistance to explain how we can be morally good—that is, if we try to deal with the moral gap without God—there are three other ways to deal with the problem that the moral demand seems too high for our natural capacities. It does not seem reasonable or even coherent to hold ourselves accountable to standards we are unable to reach. So moralists who do not want to bring God into the story try to get us to reconceptualize our situation. Either they exaggerate what our natural capacities can do, so as to make them adequate to the moral demand; or they lower the moral demand so that it fits our natural capacities; or, third, they try to find some naturalistic substitute for God's assistance in bridging the gap. This chapter will discuss each of these strategies, one section giving some background for each and the following section describing each strategy and why it fails.

Can Virtue Be Taught?

I call the first of these strategies "puffing up the capacity," like the tomato frog, *dyscophus antongilii*, which puffs itself up to twice its normal size to intimidate an opponent. I have in mind the person who says, "*Of course* we are not born with the capacity to lead a morally good life. We are not born with the capacity to speak our mother tongue either. But we are born with the capacity to respond to our parents and the other people we meet in such a way that we *learn* both the language and the moral norms. Some people learn well and some badly, in both cases. But there is no need to bring in extraordinary means like the assistance of a god in order to explain what happens here. What is going on is merely that a set of principles that society regards as normative is being internalized in people's lives through education and custom."

In 1907 a group of prominent citizens living in New York City got together once a month to discuss "the fundamentals of religion," finally publishing their conversations under the title *Talks on Religion*. The group included a mathematician, a businessperson, a historian, a philosopher, a zoologist, a student of Eastern culture, a theologian, a "social philosopher, much interested in socialism," and a banker. They disagreed about almost everything, and were amazed by the radical divergence of their views. But one thing they did agree on, and they noted this with triumph. They all agreed that society was progressing through science and universal education toward a morally better future. This belief was typical of their time.

In England, Albert Shaw wrote in 1895 about town planning, "The conditions and circumstances that surround the lives of the masses of the people in modern cities can be so adjusted to their needs as to result in the highest development of the race in body, mind and moral character. The so-called problems of the modern city are but the various phases of the one main question: How can the environment be most perfectly adapted to the welfare of urban populations? And science can meet and answer every one of these problems."

In America this kind of optimism was found notably in the philosopher and educational theorist John Dewey, especially in his earlier work. He said that the new education he was promoting was "a guarantee of a larger society which is worthy, lovely, and harmonious," and that it "has within itself the power of creating a free experimental intelligence that will do the necessary work of this complex and distracted world in which we and every other modern people have to live."

Unfortunately the century did not work out as planned. It was the bloodiest, most brutal century of human history. And this was not because of a lack of education. The people who ordered and carried out the massacres and Holocausts and ethnic cleansing were often highly cultured, cultivated people. The Jews in the concentration camps had to perform Bach for their oppressors before they were put into the gas chambers. The Germans who ran the camps may not have received a Deweyan education, but the events of the twentieth century should make us wonder about the power of education to make morally good people. Dewey was one of the original signatories of the Humanist Manifesto of 1933 (note the date, shortly before the Second World War), which stated that "man is at last becoming aware that he alone is responsible for the realization of the world of his dreams, that *he has within himself* the power for its achievement" (emphasis added). The question I am asking is whether this is true, and whether it is supported by our experience of the world run by the people who believed it. At the beginning of the new century we need to remember the lessons of the old one.

It is striking, then, that the turn of the new century is in several ways like the turn of the last one, again following a period of peace between the larger powers and the development of radically new technologies. Education theorists still hold out the hope of educational techniques that will ensure an ethical citizenry. In 1990 T. K. Stanton wrote, "The evolving pedagogy of service-learning is a key to *ensuring* the development of graduates who will participate in society actively, ethically, and with an informed critical habit of the mind" (emphasis added), and the *Journal of Moral Education* for the last decade has been full of suggestions, often referring to Dewey, for modifying the moral habits of students through educational technique. I am not attacking service-learning here. I believe in it strongly and practice it in my own teaching. When the students put faces to the issues, they change the considerations they bring to bear and improve the scope of their moral thinking. Having said that, however, I do not think that the service-learning makes the students better people; it provides an opportunity for them to become better people—an opportunity that some of them take and some of them do not.

A similar example is the teaching of medical ethics at medical school, which I have also done. There is nothing wrong with trying to get medical students to think through the ethical dimensions of the physician's life in advance, but those who promoted this idea exaggerated its potential to train ethically sensitive physicians. At the institution where I was teaching we had a medical-ethics backlash on the part of a number of the doctors who worked at the hospital. They observed that the students were not becoming ethically better doctors but were learning a fancy new terminology to justify the kind of doctoring they were going to do anyway.

Education is not unique in being perceived too optimistically as a social technique for producing virtue. This kind of overselling can be seen in many places in public life. Opponents of suburban sprawl advertise the impact of traditional town design on the virtue of the citizen body and the way sprawl produces vice. They suggest, for example, that all new developments should include a corner shop where people can buy day-to-day items without having to get into their cars. Again, limiting sprawl is an excellent idea but mismatched with some of the more passionate rhetoric used to promote it. James Kunstler, in his 1999 paper "Where Evil Dwells," talked of the effects on our souls of the American Dream of suburbia. He went on to say about the Columbine school massacre, "Teen violence is a logical response to the deep sense of purposelessness generated by the American Dream."

These ideas for education and town design are better seen more modestly, as removing some of the impediments to virtue produced by too abstract a curriculum, or by the overuse of the automobile. Immanuel Kant, in the eighteenth century, had a phrase that expresses this well. He said we should aim at "a hindrance to the hindrances to freedom." This idea is much more modest; not that we produce virtue, but that we remove impediments to it and so provide an opportunity for people to develop it if they choose. Public policy can have an impact on making some kinds of behavior habitual. But morality, as Kant also insisted, has to do with more than behavior. It has to do with motivation, with why we do what we do, and in particular with whether we give highest priority to our own happiness or to doing what is right. Service-learning, or building corner stores, may indeed change behavior for the better. But the production of the morally good heart is beyond the proper scope of public policy. We know how to remove some of the obstacles, but we do not know how to get people to actually make use of the opportunities for moral improvement we give them. You can lead the horse to water, says the proverb, but you cannot make it drink. The arrogant denial of this limitation lies behind much of the misery of the twentieth century.

Puffing Up the Capacity

In 1863 John Stuart Mill wrote in *Utilitarianism* of an "improving state of the human mind," of which the destination was a world in which "education and opinion, which have so vast a power over human character, should so use that power as to establish in the mind of every individual an indissoluble association between his own happiness and the good of the whole." Mill is making the assumption that we can produce better people by teaching and opinion shaping. Sometimes Mill's followers have suggested that if only we could be shown vividly the consequences for other people of what we do, we would tend to act in a way that promoted the good of the whole. One such philosopher is Shelly Kagan in his book *The Limits of Morality*. He points to the fact that when it comes to our own interests, we can be persuaded to visit the dentist, even if we hate dentists, by a gruesome description of an abscess and the pain it will cause us. In the same way, the vivid thought of another person's misery can persuade us to act in a way that promotes her well-being. That is why aid agencies have sponsorship programs that link up donors with particular needy children and send pictures of them; the vividness of the information makes giving money easier.

However, it does not always work this way. More information makes us more ready to help only if we were already disposed to help in the first place. If I hate somebody or am indifferent to whether he lives or dies, telling me about his need in vivid detail is not going to make me want to help him. Seeing the world through another person's eyes can make me act toward her more compassionately, but only if I care about how the world is for her. I think this is why our eyes glaze over when we read the statistics about starving children in Africa. We already know perfectly well that the need is there. We have a vestigial concern for those children, but not usually enough to make us do much about it. The battle for our lifestyle is already lost because we care most about our own comfort and convenience.

Two of Rosa's friends have been married for many years. She has watched them sadly as their relationship has declined through distrust into hatred. Each of them knows precisely how to wound the other.

Indeed they have turned this into an art form, and it provides the focus of much of their day-to-day interest in life. They are not behaving this way because they are ignorant of the hurt they are causing; in fact, the more they know the torture is working, the happier they are. In a perverse way it is their hatred for each other that keeps them together.

Puffing up the capacity is pretending that we can produce virtue in ourselves and others by some technique available to us. For Dewey the technique was a three-stage process of reflective inquiry, which he thought could be taught in school. The final stage was that "we put ourselves in the place of another, to see [these consequences] from the standpoint of [the other's] aims and values." We come to see the world from the other person's point of view. I am sure this is a good thing to encourage, and if we succeed we will have removed a kind of blindness that is an impediment to virtue. But there is something else necessary for the moral point of view. It is not enough merely to see through the other person's eyes; we have to care to make the world better for her and make her purposes and needs our own, as far as the moral law allows. The question is whether we have the capacity to produce in ourselves and others *this* kind of identification, an identification of purpose and will. The dysfunctional couple can see through each other's eyes pretty well, and each wants to produce through the eyes of the other as much pain as possible. What is more typical, though, is not hatred but indifference or very slight interest in those far away and a kind of self-preoccupation in our dealings with those close at hand.

Another example of puffing up the capacity is the suggestion that humans are reflective by nature and that reflection by itself has the tendency to bring us to a moral frame of mind. Some writers suggest that if we add merely the powers of reason and language to the capacities of nonhuman animals, this is enough to explain how humans can be morally good. A lot depends here on what is meant by "reason" or "reflection." Some accounts of these terms already build morality into them, so that it is by definition "irrational" to violate one's duty. Or sometimes "reason" is used to mean the faculty committed to all the fundamental values. These accounts make it true by definition that if we are rational, we are morally good. But unfortunately we are neither born rational in that sense, nor do we become so by some kind of statistically usual development. And if we understand reason and reflection in a morally neutral way, it remains possible to be rational, or reflective, and still a morally bad person. The defects of the Third Reich were not defects of reason, understood in this neutral way. Looking at the impeccable lists of Holocaust victims suggests more a hypertrophy or exaggeration of reason than a defect.

The first systematic treatment in Western philosophy of the question whether virtue can be taught is Plato's *Meno*, which records a dialogue between Meno and Socrates. Virtue, for Plato, is a kind of knowledge, namely, knowledge of the Form of the Good, and vice is a form of ignorance. Socrates asks in the dialogue whether it is good families that transmit virtue, or if it is good teaching methods. He points out that sometimes good families and good teaching result in virtuous young people and sometimes they don't, and he ends with the suggestion that virtue comes by divine gift. Plato was wrong, in my view, to think of vice as primarily a kind of intellectual ignorance, but he was right to think that we do not know how to produce virtue and right to hope for divine assistance. Mill and his followers have taken what is false in Plato and used it to deny what is true in him. They have started from the idea that vice is a kind of ignorance and have moved to the conclusion that we therefore know how to remove it. The Christian doctrine of original sin restrains any Dewey-style (Dewey-eyed?) optimism about unaided human capacities. But it is not necessary to believe this doctrine in order to reach this conclusion. The record of our actual failures should be enough.

Suiting the Demand to the Person

The second main strategy for bridging the moral gap without God is to keep the estimate of our natural capacities where the traditional picture of the moral gap puts it, and then to lower the moral demand so that it fits those capacities. However, this strategy fails because it lowers the demand unacceptably. The moral demand may, in some cases, be lowered appropriately. To some degree we can reasonably make different demands of different people. Jesus says, "From everyone who has been given much, much will be demanded" (Lk 12:48). Some people have great talents, have inherited great financial resources and come from supportive family backgrounds. We can appropriately expect more from them. We can also expect lower standards of musical performance from a third-year student with a Kaye cello than from a highly trained and experienced professional cellist with a Stradivarius. A performance that was pitiful from the professional could well be excellent from the student. This is also true about people's virtues and vices. But the moral demand in the organizing directive described in chapter one is the same for everyone.

Rosa's father grew up in the Great Depression, when his family lost all their wealth and were reduced to poverty. The stress was so great on his parents that they both died when he was young, and he was raised by his grandparents. This whole experience gave him an almost pathological fear of not having enough financial resources. It became extremely difficult for him to be generous with his money, even though he was moderately successful in business and had more than enough to live on. Rosa has decided that she should hold him to a lower standard because of these childhood traumas. But the lower standard is for what he actually gives, for example, to her children at Christmas. She still holds him to the same standard of thought and effort that she holds herself to; however, she knows that the same thought and effort that in her would produce a large gift, in him will produce a small one. She has lowered the external demand but held him to the same internal standard.

There can also be character specialization. Different people are better at practicing different virtues. Rosa's husband, Tom, is good at concentrating on his academic work even with distractions all round him. But he is very bad at looking after the children when he is trying to do his work at the same time. He can ignore thuds and screams from upstairs without a qualm. These are two sides of the same coin. There have been times when he knows that just because of his ability to focus, he has not been a good father. He and Rosa need to find a fair distribution of child-minding responsibilities and not pretend that he can combine the tasks. There is a kind of reduction of the demand here, being realistic about what he does well and what he does poorly. This does not mean, however, that he escapes the organizing directive described in chapter one. He cannot argue, for instance, that he has a tendency to give more weight to his own interests than impartiality allows, and therefore he should not apply the standard of impartiality to himself. He still needs to treat himself and Rosa and their children as worth the same. What is true is that the organizing directive, when applied to people with different virtue profiles, will produce different results.

Reducing the Demand

Different moral philosophers have, however, tried to lower the moral demand in each of the three parts of the organizing directive.

The first part of the directive is to judge the situation and one's response from a position that can assess and that cares most about the well-being of the whole. Some (but only some) varieties of feminist and community-emphasizing philosophy have denied this. They have urged instead the centrality of care, which we can do only with people we know about and spend a lot of time with. Thus Nel Noddings writes in her book *Caring*, "I am not obliged to care for starving children in Africa, because there is no way for this caring to be completed in the other unless I abandon the caring to which I am obligated." On this basis we can construct a response to the AIDS orphans in Zambia: "We don't have the time and resources that would enable us to care for you (we don't even know your names), and so we will stick with the people we do know (our family, friends and community)."

These philosophers have sometimes defended their position by claiming that our community makes us who we are, and we cannot step back from that community without losing our identity. If this were true, it would be nonsense to demand that people try to take a perspective that steps back from their community because this would be requiring them to become someone else. We will return to this argument in chapter nine. It fails because the community "we" belong to already contains this ideal demand for a global but also fully detailed concern for every person. Even if we agree, which I do not, that the community controls the shape of our identity, this ideal is already part of the identity we are formed with.

I grant that it is extremely difficult to reconcile our obligations to those we know with our obligations to needy strangers. This was a struggle Rosa had in the virtue profile I gave in the first chapter. To help us in this struggle, I propose a principle called "the principle of providential proximity." One thing that makes the moral demand too much to bear is that it seems to load the endless and anonymous need of the rest of the world on our pitiful shoulders as individuals. But if we can believe in providence, we can believe that we have been placed in a community that has put us next to the people that we are supposed to help. The Good Samaritan in the parable was put next to the person attacked by robbers and left wounded by the side of the road. The Greek word translated "neighbor" in that passage means literally "next to." The parable gives Jesus' answer to the question, "Who is the neighbor whom the law requires you to 'love as yourself'?" If I belong to a community that extends itself outward to meet the needs of others, if for example it sends development specialists I know to some village in Zambia, then that village becomes by extension my village. Two next-door villages can have the same needs, but one of them becomes "my" village and the other does not. I know the development specialists, or know people who know them, and the friends they make become my "friends of friends." The world's needs have in this way become less anonymous because it is now this particular village that I am responsible for and not that other one.

How do we know whom we are being put next to? Is it enough that we see a picture of a starving child in a newspaper or on the television in the evening news? I do not have a complete answer. For the Good Samaritan it was physical proximity. For us, the community we belong to (if we do belong to this kind of community) can be a significant help; it can make informed decisions about which villages to go to and which villages not. But for our community to play this role, it has to be of the right kind. It has to be both close enough to form the initial bonds that tie us in, and it has to be outward-looking enough to identify its members with their global obligations. I know that this sort of community is no longer typical and for many people will seem merely utopian.

The second part of the organizing directive is the demand to care more for people's well-being than for anything else in the world, and to bring all people equally within the scope of moral concern. There are various kinds of moral philosophy that deny we are required to recognize people's equal value in this way. Larry Arnhart in his book *Darwinian Natural Right* defends his evolutionary ethics as coming out of the most recent developments in biology and developmental psychology. He aspires to "understand human nature within the natural order of the whole." He proposes that we can make the following two identifications: the good is the desirable, and the desirable is what is generally desired by human beings. By "generally desired" he means what humans have desired throughout their evolutionary history. This gives special weight to the great length of the Pleistocene period, when evolution presumably exercised most of its effects on us. The desires evolution has given us are those that promote our survival and reproduction. When we look at human history this way, we find, Arnhart says, "that throughout most of human history, the social instincts within a tribe never extended beyond the tribe." He therefore restricts the proper scope of the commandment to "love your neighbor as yourself" to one's kin and those of one's own group, and he rejects the "universal humanitarianism" found in the Golden Rule and the parable of the Good Samaritan. He thinks he has a scientific argument from evolutionary biology for restricting care to those with whom we have special relations. I am not objecting here to the theory of evolution but to this use of it in ethics.

Arnhart concedes that we will find a "general human desire" for reciprocity, but it is only tit-for-tat, helping those who help us and harming those who harm us. If we decide we can reliably oppress some group for the foreseeable future, there is no "general human desire" given by evolution which would restrain us. The only motivation we have or morally should have, on this view, is self-interest and the interest of our own group. The oppression may be *tragic* for our victims, but Arnhart is not entitled by his theory to defend any normative standard by which we can say that such oppression is *wrong*.

This view does, indeed, reduce the ethical demand. Is this reduction legitimate? I do not think so, but it is hard to find an argument that does not beg the question. It is circular to argue that the reduction must be wrong because the ethical demand is in fact higher and does require equal concern for all human well-being as such. I think we feel the force of this higher demand, but we still have to decide whether to hold ourselves under it. And if we do, we owe some account of the authority of that demand; why should we feel that this requirement is binding on us? This is the topic of the second part of this book (chapters five to ten).

There is another use of evolutionary theory that produces the same effect as Arnhart, though by changing the status of the higher moral demand rather than by denying that we are bound by it. Some thinkers (for example, Michael Ruse in *Can a Darwinian Be a Christian?*) suppose that natural selection has given us genes for the "moral emotions" like resentment and guilt, which enable us to cooperate with each other and so produce the good things which are only possible through cooperation. Natural selection, says Ruse, gives us these genes for the sake of survival and reproductive advantage, just as it gives the cheetah speed. This means that the objective requirement we think we see in morality is an illusion produced by the genes; it is useful that we think we are under moral authority because that makes us more likely to do the things that will make us survive and breed successfully. This illusion is like a mirage: I really do think I see the pool of water in the desert, but it really isn't there. This is why I say that Ruse changes the status of the demand. His suggestion produces a lack of fit between the actual source of morality (which is self-interest) and what it feels like to us from the inside (an objective requirement to recognize the same value in any other person as in the self). But a normative theory should be able to make public what it claims as the source or origin of the moral demand without thereby undercutting the demand.

To illustrate what I mean by this, suppose we thought of the gods (as some ancient philosophers did) looking at us from their own world and being entertained by our misfortunes, just as we look at the soaps on television. Suppose, further, that the gods set us up in this world with exactly this sort of entertainment in mind. There would then be a lack of fit between the way we think of the point of our moral lives from inside them and the actual point with which the gods set us up. If we discovered that this is how things are, we might join with Shakespeare's Macbeth and say that our life is "a poor player that struts and frets his hour upon the stage," or "a tale told by an idiot, full of sound and fury, signifying nothing." What impact would this have on our lives? We would be like Sisyphus in Greek mythology, who was required by the gods to roll a rock up a mountain again and again, only to watch it roll back down again. We would shake our fists at the gods, and if we could stop the moral activity, we would.

Or suppose we discovered that morality was (as other ancient philosophers thought) programmed into us by the political elite in order to keep us subservient. Ruse's evolutionary picture puts us in this kind of situation. There is a point to our moral lives in this picture, but it is not the point we think it is from inside those lives. The Good Samaritan judges that he should help the traveler by the side of the road who has been wounded and left for dead. He thinks that what is moving him is the objective value of another person unrelated to him by kin or tribe, in fact an enemy of his own people. But according to the evolutionary picture what is actually moving him, by biochemical mechanism, is the survival and reproduction of his own genes. If we come to believe this, we will do our best to stop trying so hard to be morally good people.

There is some evidence of this in the psychological literature. When people believe that egoism is true, they are less inclined to be helpful to others. Thus a before-and-after study was done on students enrolled in two introductory economics courses and an introductory astronomy course. The students were asked at the beginning and at the end of each course what they would do if they found an addressed envelope with $100 in it. The students scored the same in the economics and astronomy courses at the beginning of the semester, but the economics students were more willing to keep the money at the end. The difference probably resulted from exposure to the theory pervasive in economics that motivation is fundamentally egoistic. I speculate that the same would be true after a semester of Professor Ruse's philosophy course.

The third part of the organizing directive is the concern for the uniqueness of each person, respecting what we do not know about someone just as much as what we know. There are many contexts in which this kind of respect is hardly possible. I worked for a couple of years on congressional staff in the House of Representatives in Washington. It is not possible for politicians as a general rule, when they are considering policy and proposing legislation, to think about the uniqueness of the people whose lives will be affected by the laws they pass. When I worked at a hospital, I observed differences between, for example, surgeons and oncologists in the degree to which they considered the individual lives (as opposed to merely the plumbing) of their patients. The oncologists had to know their individual patients well in order to determine with them what therapy was worthwhile. But these limits are not entirely fixed. Surgeons should do more by way of empathetic identification when they consult with the people they are going to cut. It is easier, to be sure, when we are dealing with people we know really well, to honor their idiosyncrasies; however, this third part of the organizing directive requires that whenever we deal with other people we try to respect their uniqueness to the degree that we can.

Some ethical theories put a disproportionate emphasis on the way we are like each other rather than the way we are different. They reduce the moral demand to what we know is the same between one human being and another. The idea of these theories is that we can draw up a list of the good things that human beings tend to pursue. Arnhart gives a list of twenty, including offspring, prestige and wealth. Another example of such a theory is the "objective list" theory of James Griffin in his book *Well-Being*. His list of values gives us a "common profile" for all human beings, and we are supposed to screen our own and other people's proposals about what to do or how to live by checking whether they are consistent with this list.

The list is supposed to be exhaustive, in the sense that it names all the main values that a normal human being would count as making a good life. One objection is that when philosophers actually give such lists, they always seem to miss things that should be there. For example, Griffin leaves out any religious values (like relationship with God) or communal values (like citizenship) from his list.

The most important objection for now, however, is different. Even if these thinkers have the common profile right, they do not adequately respect people's uniqueness. I have suggested that we each have something like an individual essence, which is equally or more valuable than our common human essence. This essence gives us values and rankings that are unique to us, and our goal is to grow into a more complete realization of that essence, even though we now know it only very imperfectly. We still have the aspirations that all humans have, and these put moral limits on how we can treat each other. But we should not think that they give us the *central* value-ordering for ourselves and all normal people. Confining the moral demand to what all humans share ends up reducing the demand to a respect for the common denominator, but not for what is most important for each individual person.

Beyond Our Control

The third strategy I mentioned for bridging the moral gap without God was to hold both the moral demand and our natural capacities where the traditional picture of the moral gap says they are, and then try to find a substitute for divine assistance in bridging the gap. Again there are many contemporary candidates for this kind of substitute. The next section will give a few brief examples. They all find hope for our salvation *within* the world and so in a sense are exaggerating our capacities, just like the first strategy. The difference is that on the third strategy the forces that produce our improvement are seen as operating beyond individual rational control.

The forces that work on us, on this view, will be larger than we are individually, and will have the power to change us in ways we cannot predict or control. But they will not be forces distinct from or transcending the universe because then they would already virtually be God. We would no longer have a strategy for bridging the moral gap without God.

Finding a Substitute

We can find several examples in social thought of the strategy of finding a substitute for God's assistance. One example is the Marxist view that if the working class took over ownership of the means of production, economic forces would produce a radical change for the better in human interrelations, to the degree that the state would wither away because it was no longer necessary. On the other side of the political spectrum there is the idea that some "invisible hand" of capitalism will transform the self-interested decisions of each into the well-being of all, but only if the magic of the marketplace is left undisturbed by external regulation. Enemies of both ideas point to the historical working out of these principles, to communism and laissez-faire capitalism, and to the evils people suffered under both of them. This is not quite fair because it supposes that the principles were in fact put into faithful practice. The supporters of both principles would now quite rightly deny this and point to compromises that were made from the very beginning. But the historical record does encourage us to doubt whether these attempts to usher in a better world through impersonal forces actually work. Wise political practice is more modest in its expectations.

Within evolutionary ethics, again, there is a proposal that plays the role of a substitute. Some thinkers want to make evolution itself a substitute for God. Perhaps this is a tendentious way to describe what they want, since the people I have in mind are theologians; they think of themselves as giving an account of God's work, not as proposing a substitute for it. Philip Hefner, in *The Human Factor: Evolution, Culture, and Religion*, identifies God as the way things really are, and since the way things really are evolves, concludes that there is evolution in God. God's transcendence, on this view, should be seen as omnipresence. In other words, God transcends any particular part of the universe and any particular time in the universe, but God does not transcend the universe itself in its spatial and temporal wholeness. Within this universe there is a direction of emergence, which the Romantics in the nineteenth century called a life force. This makes possible first the emergence of life itself, then higher forms of life, and then finally culture and freedom. Hefner supports the traditional view of the moral demand and our natural capacities. The moral demand is for self-emptying love, he says, but our natural biological tendency is to prefer the self (which he says is our sin of origin). But he thinks this gap is bridged by the self-making emergence of consciousness.

The theological difficulty with this view is that it does not take seriously enough the distinction between Creator and creature. Hefner would not agree, but he does acknowledge that he is proposing a radical revision to traditional theology. One way to put this difference is that traditional theology makes a sharp distinction between dependent and independent beings. The universe is dependent and God is independent. God can exist without the universe, but not the universe without God. In traditional theology the resources for our salvation are located not within our freedom and culture, and not within some internal force of evolution even if it is called "the evolution of God," but in the goodness of a God who creates and sustains the universe from beyond it. Traditional theology does not deny that God also dwells within the world. But it insists that this does not tell the whole story about God's existence.

This chapter has examined various contemporary examples of all three strategies for dealing with the moral gap without invoking divine assistance. I have argued that none of them are satisfactory. This does not prove that we need God's assistance; perhaps there is some other way to deal with the problem not yet mentioned. However, if the attempts described here fail, and if we cannot find another alternative, then we should go back to the traditional account that appeals to God's assistance and see if it does any better. The following chapter will look at the account that Christianity has traditionally provided.

3

God's Assistance

The previous chapter examined three strategies for dealing with the problem of the moral gap without appealing to God's assistance. I claimed that all three of them fail. Now we will see whether Christianity does any better. We will look at three doctrines about our failure to live as God calls us to live and God's assistance in overcoming this failure. An important part of this call, though not the whole of it, is to lead morally good lives. God is also calling us to lives full of aesthetic delight and to a good sense of humor. All the values that bring us closer to God are part of the call. But the lives we actually lead separate us from God, just as offenses between two human beings disrupt the relationship between them. The problem can be divided into three parts because it has three different locations in our life histories. It affects our past, our present and our future. If we are honest, we have to admit that we have lived in the past in a way that is inconsistent with God's call to us. We are continuing to do so in the present, as far as we can tell. And this looks like the case for the future, to the extent that we can do anything about it.

Christianity has the doctrines of atonement, justification and sanctification which address these three different temporal locations of the problem by proposing that God intervenes to help us. The past dimension is that we no longer need to feel the burden of unforgiven guilt for what we did in the past. The present dimension is that we have become new "in Christ," even if we cannot yet detect the difference by introspection. The future dimension is that we will change in a way we can experience, so that we gradually see ourselves becoming the sort of people God intends us to be. The history of Christian theology is full of different attempts to explain these doctrines. Being a philosopher, not a theologian, I will not try to describe this history. This chapter will look at each of the three doctrines in two sections. First, we will examine the doctrine in terms of some general concepts that are useful in understanding it, and I will raise a philosophical objection to it. Then I will defend an interpretation of each doctrine against the objection I have raised. But I am not claiming that this interpretation of the doctrines is the only way Christians can or should interpret them. Also I am not bold enough to say I have understood these doctrines except in a partial way; much remains that is mysterious about them.

Atonement

Atonement deals with the past, with the things we have done that separate us from God. Christ atoned for the sins we have committed by dying on the cross. This doctrine has at its heart the idea of forgiveness. The English word *atonement* comes (according to the *Oxford English Dictionary*) from "at-one-ment," meaning that we are reconciled or restored to unity with God. God in mercy forgives us for what we have done, and yet God also is just. I intend to defend an account of the atonement that interprets Christ's death as a punishment that Christ took so that we do not have to. But first I need to say something about what forgiveness is and what the purpose of punishment is.

Forgiveness usually involves two people: the person who has committed the offense and the person who is the victim or the target. We need to be forgiven whenever we have harmed or hurt someone, whether the offense was large or small. The process is clearest if we look at offenses within a relationship, though not all forgiveness is like this. Very often the harm is two-way, and the forgiveness has to be two-way as well. What forgiveness achieves, when it works, is that it restores the two people to the relationship they had before the offense took place. In some sense it undoes the past. This sounds mysterious, as though we could make what has happened unhappen. But this is impossible. A person can wish he had not done something stupid or hurtful, and his victim can wish he had not done it too, but neither of them can go back into the past and remove what he did from history. What the victim can do, when she forgives the offense, is to stop holding it against him and so release both of them from the burden of it.

Rosa is going to be late for work, and her daughter Lucy can't find her shoes. Rosa snaps at her that she has been careless and thoughtless, and Lucy bursts into tears. Rosa realizes that under the pressure of the time constraint she has been angrier than she should have been. She says, "I'm sorry, we'll find them together," and they both go looking. Lucy forgives her. This does not require saying to her mother "I forgive you," or saying anything at all. The two of them are close, and they both know that forgiveness has taken place. Rosa checks, though, when they find the shoes, to make sure they are completely back together. "Are you OK now?" she asks, and Lucy nods and they get into the car together to go to school.

There is a standard pattern for how this process works. The offender repents, apologizes, makes the damage good, and then the victim releases her or him. It is important that forgiving is not the

same as overlooking the offense or condoning it. Something wrong
has been done, and forgiveness requires acknowledging that it was
wrong. This is where God's justice comes in. Whatever else atonement accomplishes, it does not mean that God somehow does not
mind the offense. That would not be consistent with God's justice or
righteousness, which is unalterably opposed to sin. Also forgiveness is
not the same as forgetting the offense, as though God could erase the
divine knowledge of what the offender has done. Rather, God ceases
to remember the offense *against* the offender. The offender may also
remember what he has done, since it has shaped his own life. But
after God forgives him, he no longer needs to see the offense as an
obstacle to his relation with God. One picture of this is that there is a
book in heaven listing all our misdeeds, with one column for the
misdeeds and one for the penalties. When God forgives us, the misdeeds stay in the book, but the penalty column is erased.

Atonement requires making good the offense. Sometimes this is
done by punishment. We punish crime for various different reasons.
Perhaps we do it as a deterrent. People who know they are likely to
suffer if they are caught committing a crime are less likely to do the
crime in the first place. Or perhaps we lock people up in order to
keep them off the streets. Or maybe we think we can make people
better by training them in a healthy environment, so that they will be
less likely to repeat their offenses when they go back into society.
These are all forward-looking justifications for punishment.

There is one kind of justification which is backward looking. It
says that we punish offenders because they deserve to be punished
after what they have done, and the degree of the punishment needs
to fit the degree of the offense. This is how the offenders, to the best
of their ability, make the damage good and "pay their debt to society." I think a variant of this approach is right (though the other
approaches also have merit, some more than others). Taking an eye
for an eye is not itself something good. In this sense we can agree that

two wrongs (or two harms) do not make a right (or a good). But punishment is important because it expresses the value of the victim. The bully on a school playground demeans his victim. He expresses by taunting him and beating him up that the victim is worth next to nothing. The bully's punishment reverses this. It expresses the moral truth that the two of them are both humans, with equal value. It raises the standing of the victim by lowering the standing of his tormenter. I call this "the expressive theory of punishment."

Punishment is one way for the offender to make amends, even if he or she has no desire or intention to do so. Is forgiveness possible without the offender making amends? I think so, but this is controversial. Sometimes the offender has done something for which no punishment could make adequate amends. If he has raped a woman, for example, he can repent and say he is sorry, but there is nothing he can do to make it up to her (even if society kills him). I think we can still forgive, even where the offender has done nothing to remove the offense. In the end it benefits us to release the burden of hatred we have, though this is a personal matter and other people will not usually know the right timing. More than that, in Christianity the teaching is that we *should* forgive or at least ask God to forgive. For example, Christ on the cross asks his father to forgive those who are crucifying him even though they have not repented. Sometimes we can release the forgiveness into God's hands even where we cannot yet do the forgiveness ourselves. Still, if the victim forgives where there is no "making amends" or reparation, or even any repentance, she has to bear an additional burden. Sometimes, indeed, it is as though the victim has to pay twice, paying the offender's share herself. She has to pay the first time, when the offense is committed, and then she has to pay a second time when she recognizes that she cannot be paid back but decides she will forgive anyway. In the case of Christ's atonement, he takes the punishment for our sins instead of us.

To what extent is Christ's atonement like human forgiveness and punishment? One philosophical objection to the atonement is that it is not possible to hand over guilt, as though it were a financial debt, from one person to another. With money it is possible for one person to take over debt from another. But does it make sense to say that one person can take guilt from another? If we understand atonement as substitution, are we saying that Christ became guilty of our sins? If not, then how can God justly punish Christ if he is innocent? One idea that can help us here is the idea of a partial merger of identity between two people.

Partial Mergers of Identity

Partial mergers of identity between two people are a familiar part of our experience. There are various contexts in human life where fault is shared from one person to another. The following example was already mentioned in chapter one.

When Ned was a baby, Rosa took him to visit her pastor, who wanted to hold him. The pastor took him against his shoulder with an air of confidence, supporting him with one hand and patting his back with the other. Ned promptly spit up on his shirt. What did Rosa do? She behaved just as if she had vomited herself. She was terribly sorry, she apologized, she seized back her baby and offered to pay for the shirt to be cleaned. Why is this? It is because she and her baby formed a unit together. He had been, until very recently, inside her, and she was still feeding him from her own body. She went everywhere with him, almost as though he were an extension of herself; and when people said how adorable he was, she was proud of him and proud of herself and proud (most accurately) of the both-of-them-together as a single unit.

Here we have to the greatest degree an identification between two people. John Donne, the seventeenth-century poet, puts this by making up a word, *interinanimate,* which means to put a new soul (anima) into (in) the space between (inter) two people.

> When love with one another so
> Interinanimates two souls,
> That abler soul which thence doth grow
> Defects of loneliness controls.

This kind of partial identification can happen between a husband and wife, so that each can be ashamed or proud of what the other does. Tom, Rosa's husband, once made a fool of himself at work by telling a lie about his previous job, which was then exposed. He and Rosa both felt they had to go into hiding for a few weeks. The shame spread to the both-of-them-together, and this was a sign that some kind of fault had also spread. This partial merging can happen between colleagues who are loyal to each other and to the institution they both belong to. In fact, at some religiously based academic institutions new faculty members are asked to subscribe to old catechisms or confessions, with a context in centuries-old battles about doctrine and practice. The result of this is to make them part of the community with its particular history. They can become proud of some things in that history and ashamed of other things; in the same way the current membership of the community is both proud and ashamed.

It may sound odd to talk of one person being ashamed or proud of what another person has done. However, this is in fact a familiar part of our experience with the kind of partial identification I am talking about. This kind of sharing of fault and therefore of the corresponding emotions is appropriate to the degree that the partial merger of identity is appropriate. Certainly they can both be inappropriate, as when two people become codependent and lose a proper sense of their own identities. But these partial mergers are often good for us, and in fact they constitute a significant part of a happy human life.

I am proposing that we think of the unity between the believer and Christ as one of these partial mergers of identity. John Calvin talks about a "mystical union." This means we can think of a kind of two-way transfer. There is a transfer from the believer to Christ and a transfer from Christ to the believer. A useful picture here is that of a child being adopted into a family. There can be the same kind of transfer in both directions, from the new child to its new family and from the family back to the child. Adoption is a picture used in the New Testament for the way we are incorporated into Christ's family as his brothers and sisters. So we should think of a similar two-way transfer with Christ; our failures are shared with him, and his kind of life is shared with us. Atonement is the first part of this. Because Christ takes our sins, he can take the punishment for them. Because we become joined to Christ, there is a transfer back to us of Christ's kind of life, and through us this life is then shared with others.

Rosa's brother and his wife adopted an eight-year-old boy, Chad, into their family. Chad had a troubled history and started to get into the same kind of trouble at his new school. He stole from other students' lockers. By the adoption and so the partial merger of identity, these failures became failures of the whole family and all its members were painfully ashamed of them, especially Chad's new older brother who was at the same school. But because of the same partial merger, a transfer started back to Chad of the kind of life that the family had always lived together. They respected each other and each other's property, and Chad began to be proud of his new identity. He learned from the respect and love that he was given how to respect and love other people. He was learning how to live out the new life that had already become his by adoption into his new family.

My aim is to give some suggestive analogies. These examples do not solve all the difficulties about the atonement. However, the ideas of partial merger and two-way transfer are helpful in understanding this complex doctrine.

Justification

The doctrine that we are justified in Christ concerns our present standing before God. Sometimes the teaching is put this way: God sees us "in Christ" and so does not count our imperfections as part of our new identity. God counts us as righteous. The word *justify* literally means "make just," and the sense of "just" here is very broad, including all the components of righteousness or a life pleasing to God.

How are we to understand God's help here? God does not count us as righteous because we have become virtuous inside, on the version of the doctrine given here. Nor is God responding to a change outside us, as though we were draped in a white robe which hid our flaws from view (this is not how to understand Rev 6:11). That would be odd because how could anything hide itself from God's view? Isn't God supposed to be omniscient? It is natural to be baffled at this point and to object that there is no doctrine here to help with the moral gap at all. Christians go on sinning. The doctrine was supposed to help with this gap between the moral demand and our natural capacities. But if there is not a change inside or outside, where is the present help supposed to be?

The version of the doctrine of justification outlined here replies that God sees us already in a way we are not yet. Part of what is mysterious here is God's relation to time. I will not try to explain this because I do not know how. But here are three analogies from human experience that show other contexts in which to understand the combination of "already" and "not yet."

Already and Not Yet

There are several places in human life in which we experience the strange combination of both being in process toward something and in some sense already there.

The first example is from the experience of becoming an American citizen, which I have done. The candidates take a test and swear an oath before a judge, and then the judge declares them citizens. The judge's declaration produces an immediate change of status, even though there has not yet been an internal change. The new citizens do not yet find baseball intuitively appealing or resonate to country western music. There is no external change either (except perhaps some signatures somewhere or some spoken promises; but those are not the new reality itself, only signs of it). The candidates do not become citizens by being draped from that time onward in the stars and stripes. Nonetheless the change in status is real.

Some might deny this, insisting that the only reality is what can be experienced then and there. They might say that the words of the citizenship oath are real because they can be heard, but there is no real change in the candidates until they have changed inside; until then the American-ness is just a legal fiction because the kind of life that is characteristically American is not yet in place. However, I think this is the wrong way to look at it. Changes can be real even though they cannot be experienced yet. In this kind of case we have an "already" and a "not yet." After some years of living out the new citizenship, there will probably be internal and external changes. To their own surprise the new citizens may find themselves deeply moved at a time of national tragedy by a sense of solidarity with their fellow citizens. But these changes are not necessary for the change of status. After the oath they have changed in reality; they are already citizens.

Another example is from music. I am thinking as I write this of the opening of Beethoven's *Fifth Symphony* (ta ta ta tum), but the point applies to most pieces of any significant scope. A theme or phrase is stated once, and then this motif becomes more and more significant as it is repeated in different contexts, modified and turned into a longer theme, played by different instruments high and low and separate and together. If we ask what the meaning of this motif is, the answer is given by the whole piece. If the same sequence of notes is used in an advertising jingle, it means something different. The complex development is already implicit the first time the notes are played, even though the first occurrence may be simple and apparently naive. The first statement of the theme has the "already and not yet" character that I am trying to identify.

Consider the experience of listening to a piece of music we already know and love. We hear those initial notes this time around, and there is a heightened excitement, a pregnancy, given by what we already know is going to happen to the phrase in the rest of the piece. And yet we can hear the progression of the movement and still be delighted by the changes in it. Are we deceiving ourselves when we experience this kind of pleasure? Do we pretend to ourselves that we do not know yet how the piece is going to turn out? This does not seem right as a description of what happens to us. It is rather that the phrase at the beginning is simultaneously experienced as new and as familiar. It already has the special significance that the development of the whole piece gives it, and yet physically (as our ears receive it) it is merely "ta ta ta tum," no more and no less. I admitted before that I do not understand God's relation to time. But it may be that it permits the same kind of double truth, or something analogous to it. God knows us both as we will be eventually and as we are in each of the stages that we experience as successive, one after another. We do not yet see the meaning of our lives as God already sees it.

A third example, and I think the most helpful, comes from biology. An acorn does not yet look much like an oak tree, and yet it is already fully oak. (Chapter seven will return to this example and say more about some of the difficulties with it.) We have recently been able to locate some of the genetic mechanisms that produce the development. There is a certain kind of unity through change that only substances have. We understand the world most basically in terms of individual substances and what happens to them. This is how we sort out our sense impressions of the world into a relatively orderly pattern. A heap of sand is not an individual substance because there is no answer to the question, "Is it the same heap when I take away a grain, or two grains, or three grains?" There is no principle or essence of "heapness" which could give us an answer. The same is true with a puddle, and the water that gradually evaporates from it. Heaps of sand and puddles of water do not have the kind of unity or internal organizing principle required for being an individual substance.

However, the acorn does have it, and it is the same kind of unity as the oak tree. What constitutes this unity is the kind of life the acorn has, and to understand this kind of life we need to see its eventual realization in the oak tree. When we see such a tree, we know that there is an individual substance there and that it has some characteristic kind of life and some process of normal development that has led to it. We think of the tree as a basic constituent of the world, around which we can organize the jumble of our initial sensations. But this knowledge allows us to think of the acorn as already a substance, though it is not yet a tree. Here also we have an "already" and a "not yet." Theologically the point is that God looks at our final realization and that is what defines us as the individual substance that we are. The first chapter put this in terms of the name that God has for us, written on a white stone; the name discloses what each one of us is. But God does not have to wait to give us the name until we get to heaven. The name is already there even though we do not yet live up to it.

These three analogies are intended to help us understand the doctrine of justification. The objection was that this doctrine does not answer the problem of the moral gap. Christians who have been justified still sin. So justification does not seem to close the gap. But if we can begin to understand how God can see us already as we are not yet, we can also begin to understand how the gap can be already closed even though we experience ourselves as not yet good in the way we are supposed to be. The closing of the gap is our destination, and God sees that destination as making us the individual persons that we are.

What does this have to do with Christ? Christ was obedient in one way when he was put to death on the cross for our sins. But he was also obedient by keeping the law in a way that reveals to us how we should live. He had the kind of love for his Father and for his neighbors that sums up all the commandments of the law. His life is in this way a model for us. But it is not merely a model. It is a life into which we are incorporated by the kind of partial merger of identity discussed earlier in the chapter. Through our adoption we now belong as brothers and sisters to the family that is characterized by this kind of love, and through us this love can extend itself to other people.

Sanctification

If justification is about our present, the doctrine of sanctification as I shall interpret it (acknowledging that there are other Christian interpretations) has essential reference to our future. The word *sanctify* literally means "make holy." In the version of the doctrine I am trying to explain, this "making holy" is something we experience over time. It is a process. In terms of the analogy of becoming an American citizen, this would be the process of Americanization, which those who come to stay gradually undergo. The first section of this chapter talked about a two-way transfer, like that between an adopted child and his adoptive family. Sanctification is the second transfer, of Christ's life back to us, as our lives gradually become more like his.

Does this mean that the lives of all those who are being sanctified become more and more the same? This is not quite right. A poem by Gerard Manley Hopkins expresses this well. I will explain some of the more difficult lines in a moment.

As kingfishers catch fire, dragonflies draw flame;
As tumbled over rim in roundy wells
Stones ring; like each tucked string tells, each hung bell's
Bow swung finds tongue to fling out broad its name;
Each mortal thing does one thing and the same:
Deals out that being indoors each one dwells;
Selves—goes itself; *myself* it speaks and spells,
Crying *What I do is me: for that I came.*

I say more: the just man justices;
Keeps grace: that keeps all his goings graces;
Acts in God's eye what in God's eye he is—
Christ—for Christ plays in ten thousand places,
Lovely in limbs, and lovely in eyes not his
To the Father through the features of men's faces.

Hopkins was much influenced by Duns Scotus, a Franciscan philosopher of the fourteenth century who also worked in Oxford. Scotus taught that individuals have individual essences, which are more perfect than the human essence that we all share. This was the third part of the organizing directive discussed in the first chapter, the direction to love each other's uniqueness at least as much as what we have in common.

In the first stanza of his poem Hopkins starts with two images from what we can see and three from what we can hear. Kingfishers in Britain are not like those in the United States. They are small and turquoise, and like dragonflies they flash in the sun. Both creatures take the gleam from the sun and send it back changed by the luster of their own vivid feathers or skin. Dropping a stone into a well, and plucking a string and swinging a bell with the pull of a bell-rope—each of these releases a sound that becomes more than itself as it spreads and yet at the same time reveals the special character of the rock hitting the water or the vibrating gut or the struck bronze. Each flings out its name, and so the particular being or essence that dwells inside it. It "selves." And in this "selving" it fulfills its purpose, the point of its existence.

In the second stanza Hopkins says more, that the just (the righteous) man is given grace by God, so that he acts in a way that reflects what he already is in God's eyes, namely, Christ. This is a reference to the doctrine of justification. Does this mean that we are all the same because we are all Christ? Yes and no, the poem says. Every life that is "in Christ" has the character of Christ's life and is lovely in God the Father's eyes as Christ is lovely. But the features of the faces are ours and unique to each one of us. This is the variety "in Christ," and God loves this variety.

A story in the New Testament (Lk 8:40–56) gives an example of what this might mean in moral life. Jairus was ruler of the local synagogue, accustomed to a conspicuous and leading role in public life. But his twelve-year-old daughter was dying, and there was nothing he could do to prevent it. As a last resort, and as a concession to the authority of another, he came to Jesus to ask for help, and Jesus was willing.

However, they were interrupted as they walked back to the house, surrounded by crowds. A woman who had suffered for twelve years from hemorrhages, and so was unclean by Jewish law, had touched one of the fringes on Jesus' cloak and was immediately healed. Jewish law prescribed these fringes as a memorial to the commandments, one of which forbade Jesus to touch her, but which were summed up in the commandment to love. She too wanted healing from him. But she could not ask for it openly, for he could not touch her without becoming unclean himself; thus she hoped to do it secretly through his garment. However, Jesus would not let her escape notice. He asked who had touched him, and at first she denied it, along with everyone else. But when she saw that she could not remain hidden, she overcame twelve years of shame and told the whole crowd not just what she had done but why, and how she had been healed.

Meanwhile Jairus was waiting, the hardest thing in the world for him with his daughter on the verge of death. And while Jesus was making time for the woman to reveal herself to the crowd, a servant came and told Jairus that his daughter was dead. Jairus could have turned his back on Jesus in despair and anger. But Jesus told him to believe and his daughter would be saved. Jairus allowed him to take over, to rebuke the mourners at the house, to take the dead girl's hand (again making himself unclean) and call her back to life.

In this story Jesus asks two people to face opposite temptations or characteristic weaknesses. Jairus has to overcome the temptation of the strong to self-sufficiency; he has to wait, to subordinate himself to Jesus' leading. The woman has to face the temptation of the weak to hide; she has to become public, to reveal herself and her humiliation. Should we say that Jesus wants them to become the same, to approach some generic best shape of virtue from the positions of too much and too little pride of status? That is not quite right. Rather, each has to grow into the name or the nature that "indoors each one dwells." And the path to this is straight through what is hardest for each one. Each has to be, as it were, broken open. Hopkins uses such an image in another poem, perhaps his greatest, "The Windhover." We have to suffer in the way a charred piece of wood left at the end of a long-burning fire finally breaks open to reveal the glow of the flame at its heart, "and blue-bleak embers, ah my dear, fall, gall themselves, and gash gold-vermilion."

How does sanctification work? What is its mechanism? These are in a way foolish questions; we are talking about a work of God, and we should not expect to know how God works. But theology points to the Holy Spirit, who convicts us, counsels us and comforts us. The Holy Spirit brings to our minds our deficiencies, calls us to the path we need to follow and gives us strength to follow it (*comfort* means originally "strengthen"). Do we therefore see ourselves improving? Here the story is mixed. Those who seem to the outside eye to be far advanced on the path of holiness often seem to themselves to be full of sin. This is mysterious. But perhaps what happens is that some temptation that used to be hard becomes easier to resist, and this reveals underneath it some other temptation that is hard (for example, self-congratulation at resisting the first temptation). So that there is always sin to be faced, and sin is always abhorrent. Some theologians say that all sin is equally abhorrent; that seems to me an overstatement. In any case, it is possible for there to be real improvement without the sense of being at all close to holiness or purity, and this combined state of progress and self-reproach seems to be typical of the greatest saints. Sanctification is getting closer to the particular splendor that God sees in us, even though we do not yet see it.

There is a natural objection to the doctrine. Surely moral growth is something we do, not something that is caused in us from the outside. But I have talked about sanctification as the work of the Holy Spirit, convicting, counseling and comforting. The objection is that if it really is the work of God in us, then we become merely the material in which the process takes place; but this takes away our freedom and our responsibility, and we are not left with anything recognizably moral at all. The idea of a partial merger of identity suggests a response to this objection.

Partial Mergers Again

Here, as in most of this chapter, I am dealing with mysteries I do not claim to understand in full. The present mystery is the cooperation in our growth between God's agency and our own. I think it is helpful (though it does not remove all the difficulties) to go back to the idea of a partial merger of identity mentioned in the first section of this chapter, and to look again at the various analogies drawn there. In a purely human context moral growth is a joint enterprise, and we have the same difficulty in sorting out who is doing what. But this difficulty in the human context should not tempt us to deny our

freedom or responsibility. The same is true in the context of our relation to God, even though (as I shall say at the end) God's initiative in
the relation makes it different from our human relations to one
another.

Lucy grows morally through the episode of the lost shoes. She can
see she has caused her mother distress by not being careful about
where she put her shoes when she took them off the night before. If
she loves her mother, this distress is also her own distress. That is
partly why she cries. She could not explain it this way, but it is nonetheless true that the distress is dumped on her from her mother.
Rosa, on her side, is not merely cross at her daughter but also cross at
herself about the losing of the shoes. Partly this is a kind of flashback
to her youth, where she has vivid memories of just this kind of thing
happening to her as well. Indeed she finds that she gets most cross at
her children exactly at the times they display her own weaknesses,
and her anger is directed as much against herself as against them.
When she sees Lucy crying, she is moved by her distress, and there is
a kind of reverse dumping. When she apologizes, she is in fact saying
that she is sorry for the whole mess, to which they have both con-
tributed in various ways that cannot be completely sorted out; when
her daughter forgives her, she is forgiving the whole mess, and both
of them are involved mutually in every stage of this.

We systematize the episode into two offenses, one by Lucy (losing
her shoes) and one by Rosa (snapping at her daughter), and two acts
of forgiveness. But this is an oversimplification. Both offenses and
both acts of forgiveness involve both of them. Lucy has grown
through all of this. She has become more like what God sees her
already to be. But how much of this growth is done by her and how
much by Rosa? I am not trying to say that Rosa and her daughter
become one person. No doubt partial merger can in some cases go
too far, and there can be a loss of self that is dangerous or even pathological. But this is not the case I am imagining. The two of them are

different people, and yet growth by one of them is equally growth by
the two of them considered as a unit, a development (to use Donne's
language again) of the "abler soul" that grows between them. They
get back together, and the unit is stronger than it was before.

When we fail, we grieve the Holy Spirit (Eph 4:30). When we are
in pain and we pray, we sometimes cannot find the words, but the
Spirit "intercedes with sighs too deep for words" (Rom 8:26). When
we suffer, we "share Christ's sufferings" (1 Pet 4:13), so that through
the partial merger he is suffering with us. This is not to say that the
Holy Spirit grows with us in sanctification. The Holy Spirit is already
holy and has no need to grow. But the growth and development is
nonetheless a growth in the unit that is formed between us, and we
should not expect to be able to sort out what is done by each party
any more than we can with Rosa and her daughter. The growth, we
might say, is something done by the both-of-them, and the character
of the unit formed is unique to the both-of-them. After we have
grieved the Spirit and repented, sometimes in the Spirit's own power,
the unit formed between us is stronger. And then it is better able to
do the work in Christ's whole body that it is called to do.

One defect of the analogy of Rosa and Lucy will be stressed by
Calvinists. If we apply it to the relation between God and us, it does
not give God the right kind of initiative. By the three doctrines I
have discussed in this chapter, God the Father chooses to adopt us,
Christ chooses to die for us, and the Holy Spirit chooses to enter
into us, though I have not tried to establish any order among these
divine choices. I think the initiative question is different from the
question of whether moral growth is something we do or whether
we are just the material in which the process takes place. I think God
initiates the process in which the body grows, and the choosing we
do during this growth is part of this same process. God starts in us the
kind of restlessness that leads us in the end back to God. However, I
do not pretend to understand how all of this fits together. I have

merely made the modest point that we have the same kind of difficulty sorting out who does what in human affairs. Chapter ten returns to the nature of human autonomy and restlessness.

This chapter has looked at some of the resources in Christian doctrine for understanding how we can be reconciled to God despite our failures to live by God's call to us. We can find some help in understanding how the moral gap could be bridged. We can believe in atonement—that we are forgiven for the wrong we have done, even though not by our own deserving. We can believe in justification—that God already sees us as righteous even though we are not yet living in the way we are called to live. We can believe in sanctification—a gradual process of becoming closer to holiness, even though we are more and more aware of our imperfection. These three doctrines remain mysterious in different ways; however, this is a reason to try to understand them as much as we can, not to abandon them in despair. All three doctrines concern our inside lives, our hearts. We also have to believe something about the outside world in which we live if we are to sustain the moral life. That is the topic of the next chapter, which is about the doctrine of providence.

4

Providence

What do we need to believe as moral agents about the world in which we live? Our focus here will be the doctrine of providence and how it relates to morality. The basic idea is that if we are going to persevere in the moral life, we have to believe that the world makes moral sense, even though we also have to recognize the evil and tragedy that we and other people experience. We cannot simply say, with Shakespeare's Macbeth, that our life is a tale full of sound and fury, signifying nothing. But we also cannot simply say, with Voltaire's Dr. Pangloss, that all is for the best in the best of all possible worlds.

A good place to begin is the idea of moral faith, which I first learned from Immanuel Kant. This idea has two components, the faith that it is possible for us to be morally good in our hearts and the faith that the world outside us makes moral sense. The first of these two components was the topic of chapter three. We examined the Christian doctrines of atonement, justification and sanctification in order to explain how Christianity thinks of God's assistance. Moral people have to believe that their capacities have been transformed *inside* themselves. The second component of moral faith is that the world *outside* is the kind of place in which happiness is reliably connected with a morally good life. To put this the other way around, moral people need to believe that they do not have to do what is morally bad in order to be happy. When I say "they need to," I mean that they need to if they want a coherent view. Perhaps many people do not even ask themselves the question. But this belief is nonetheless implicit in how they go about their lives.

We will start by considering the way in which morally good people should be concerned with their happiness. I will then construct an argument that we need to believe that virtue and happiness go together in the long run. In the following section I will add that we need to believe this even if we do not believe that most other people are virtuous. This brings us in the next section to the need for moral faith in providence, which is a kind of *faith* because it cannot be proved from experience. The chapter ends with a discussion of how providence can come to us through our history, not merely in the present circumstances of our lives.

Happiness and Morality

Providence, as I shall use the term in this chapter, is an ordering behind or within the universe, which allows it to make moral sense in the following way: people who have faith in providence believe their happiness is reliably connected with their attempt to be morally good, and they can see that this same connection works for everyone. They believe that nobody's happiness depends on their doing what is morally wrong—what violates the organizing directive—or on their refusing to do what is morally right.

Rosa's brother and sister-in-law made the decision to adopt Chad when he was eight years old. This was a hard decision because he had already been in trouble and had been through more than one foster home. They considered the needs of the other members of their family and talked with them often and carefully about the decision. They thought about times in the past when they had been obedient to what seemed right, even though it was hard, and remembered how they had been blessed. In the end, even though they knew they were taking a risk, they decided it was the right thing to do; they had the faith that this would be good for Chad and consistent with the well-being of their whole family.

This notion of providence does not mention God. It does not say that God supervises the world and brings about the proportioning of virtue and happiness. I think it is a separate and important question whether morality as we are familiar with it requires believing that the moral order has a *person* behind it who does the ordering. The idea that there is a moral order is vaguer. I think it is part of what we tend to believe whether we are believers in God or not. I am not claiming, however, that this idea has been part of every culture in the world's history. In Homer's world, the heroes do not consider the consistency of their way of life with the virtue and happiness of all human beings.

Believing in providence does not mean that we view moral goodness as a means to our happiness. That would be inconsistent with a proper respect for morality, for respecting morality means not subordinating it to our own happiness. I need to say more about this, for there is one strong tradition that would deny it. This tradition follows the views of Plato and Aristotle, who had a theory of motivation according to which everything that we desire comes under the general heading of our own happiness. Happiness, on this view, is the chief good for each person, and this chief good incorporates all our ends and goals and purposes, which are either components of our happiness or means toward it. Even virtue is included here, so that it is our own happiness that motivates us toward virtue. This view of motivation does not mean that we are always selfish. Aristotle, for example, allows that a person can include other people in his or her happiness. Thus parents' happiness includes the well-being of their children, and friends' happiness includes the well-being of their friends. This is because, Aristotle says, the child becomes "another self" for the parent, and the friend becomes "another self" for his friend. The "me-self" becomes a "we-self." Our skin becomes, so to speak, elastic, so that we can fit more and more people inside it, and regard their happiness as part of our own. We are motivated to help these other people "for their sake," on this view, but only because they have become identified with us. If we lose this identification, we lose the motivation along with it.

A different view of human motivation is proposed by John Duns Scotus, who emphasized the self-emptying character of Christian love for God and neighbor. Scotus says that we humans have two fundamentally different kinds of motivation, one toward our own happiness and one toward what is good in itself (for example, God) independently of our happiness. He thinks we are free only because we have this second kind of motivation. He distinguishes here between freedom and nature. Our desire for our own happiness or perfection is given us by nature and is not something we choose. Nonhuman animals do not choose whether to put themselves (and their own kin and group) first; they do this automatically. But humans have the freedom to prefer what is good in itself, independently of any relation to their own happiness. The Good Samaritan helped even an enemy of his own people who had fallen wounded by the side of the road. For generations Presbyterian clergy at the close of their ordination service declared their willingness to be damned for the sake of the glory of God, and they were echoing words of Moses and Paul (see Ex 32:32 and Rom 9:3). So humans have these two kinds of motivation. The doctrine of the Fall is that we are born with the wrong ranking of them, with the desire for our own happiness first and the love for what is good in itself second.

Like Scotus, I believe that we can love the good for its own sake, and not as part of our own happiness. However, it is consistent with this to care about whether a commitment to what is good in itself will lead to our happiness. We are the kind of creatures who do in fact care about this, and there is nothing wrong with that. The background in Christian doctrine is that we were created that way, and God wants us to be happy even more than we want it. Even in heaven, Scotus says, we will care about our own happiness. The key question, however, is the ranking of these two different motivations. Which do we put first, our happiness or the good in itself? The right frame of mind, I am claiming, is to put the good first but still care about whether pursuing the good will make us happy. There is a danger in this frame of mind. For it is easy to deceive ourselves and think we are pursuing the good in itself when actually it is our happiness all the time that is motivating us.

I remember, for example, visiting a Christian elementary school that had a student project displayed on the walls. The students had drawn pictures with two halves, a top and a bottom divided by a line. On the bottom were drawings of good deeds, like helping with the washing-up. On the top were pictures of heaven, with Jesus holding out his arms in welcome. The message of the project was that if you did the kind of thing shown in the bottom half, you would get the reward shown in the top half. And there is nothing wrong, I think, with the belief that those who live in a way that pleases God will end up in heaven, though they are not saved by their works. The tricky question is about motivation. Perhaps God is merciful to us and does not mind if we start out wanting to be good in order to go to heaven. However, if this remains the basic structure of our motivation, I think there is something wrong with it.

Moral faith is the faith that being good is consistent with our own happiness. But believing this requires faith that there is something (or someone) holding our love for the good in itself and our happiness together. Our happiness is not simply being virtuous but involves enough other goods to give us a good life. The Christian background for moral faith is the belief that if we seek first the kingdom of God and his righteousness, we will receive these other things as well (see Mt 6:33 and Ps 37:4). However, I am arguing here that this belief in providence is part of "our" moral picture whether we are believers in God or not. The question for this chapter is why a moral agent should need this kind of moral faith in providence at all.

Self-Rewarding Morality

This section will argue that we need to believe in what I will call "self-rewarding morality"; then the next section will try to show that this belief is not enough—that we need to believe in providence as well. Self-rewarding morality is a system in which everyone's virtue is what makes everyone happy. I will start by showing that "we" do think that if we were all morally good, we would almost all be happy. This belief is woven into the fabric of morality as we are familiar with it, and cannot be torn out without substantial damage to that fabric. Consider the following two beliefs that people engaged in the moral life need to have about their own lives. They have to believe that they can be good people. The previous three chapters have underscored how hard it is to believe this. The second thing they have to believe, I think, is that they can usually bring about the good things they try to bring about. I will call this their "effectiveness belief." They have to believe this because otherwise there would be no point in trying to bring those good things about.

Imagine an evil genius with enormous power to manipulate our lives. Suppose he brought it about that whenever we tried to do good we ended up doing harm. I think we would stop trying to do good; there would be no point to it. So we have to believe that there is no such evil genius, that the world is not like that, and that we can actually do the good we set out to do. It is not enough that when we try to do good, good usually happens; this could be mere coincidence. We have to believe that the good result we achieve is what we planned and that it came about through our planning to achieve it.

Rosa went to the library to take out a book for her work. She picked the wrong volume from the shelves and was about to return it when she saw an envelope stuck into the middle. Curious, she opened it up and found an airline ticket for a flight that very evening, with the purchaser's address on the envelope. She hurried to find a phone book and was able to contact him before he left. He had not even realized that the ticket was not securely in his travel wallet. She tried to do good (to take out the book) and she achieved good (returning the ticket). She even thought there might be something providential about the whole episode. But if this is the way her actions are usually connected with the good, she will stop planning or deliberating. She will assume that some invisible hand is guiding her into these paths, and there is no point in thinking ahead about what those paths might be. To persevere in the moral life, she needs to believe that the good she achieves is the good she *tries* to achieve.

People engaged in the moral life need to have beliefs not only about their own lives but about the lives of other people as well. They have to believe that others can be good people, and they need to have an effectiveness belief about others, that others can also usually bring about the good things they try to bring about. Why do we have to believe that other people can be morally good? One answer to this is that morality requires us to think of each other that way. Moral people have to respect other people. This idea is implied in the organizing directive described in chapter one. This does not mean moral people have to regard other people as actually virtuous. But they cannot respect others if they do not regard them as capable of virtue.

Christian doctrine has an additional point here, which takes us beyond what is shared by Christians and non-Christians. How does the capacity for virtue turn into actual virtue? Augustine says, "God bids us do what we cannot, that we may know what we ought to seek from him." This looks strange at first. Augustine seems to be saying that God holds us accountable to a standard we are unable to reach. But the point is that we are only unable to reach this standard if we are on our own, without God's assistance. To hold that "ought" implies "can" does not require holding that "ought" implies "can all on our own" or "can by our own devices." God is holding us accountable, in the traditional picture, to standards that we can reach, but only with the help offered to us.

Luther illustrates this by an analogy. He says that God is like a parent who tells a small child to walk toward him. The child cannot do this yet, but she stands up, takes a step or two and starts to totter. The parent then holds out his hands so that the child can grab hold of them and walk the next few steps with his assistance. To respect another person requires believing that she has enough good in her so that given the assistance that is in fact available (including God's assistance), she can be a good person. I say "that is in fact available" because I do not mean merely "given the assistance that could possibly be available." What we think someone is capable of will depend on what kind of assistance we think is actually available. Christians believe that God does actually offer help with leading a morally good life.

Now we can return to what is shared between Christians and non-Christians. People engaged in the moral life need to have the effectiveness belief about other people that others can usually bring about the good things they try to bring about. Why do moral people have to believe this? Our intentions are massively interconnected with other people's intentions. It is hard to think of any intention I might have that does not require me to trust that others have the ability to carry out most of the good things they choose to do. Consider, for example, the intention that I formed to write this book. Think of all the hundreds of other people whose intentions and actions were involved in my carrying out this plan: the people who avoided my car on the highway, the people who made and sold me my computer, the people who shelved books in the library, the copy-editors at the publishing house and so on. Then think of the hundreds of thousands involved in *those* people's intentions being fulfilled. Throw a stone into the pool, and eventually the ripples reach the edge, the whole human race. This means that I cannot believe that I can bring about what I am undertaking unless I believe that this is true of other people as well.

If we add together these two beliefs about other people, we get the belief in self-rewarding morality that we started with. Self-rewarding morality is a system in which our own and other people's virtue produces our own and other people's happiness. Suppose everyone not merely could be virtuous but was virtuous; and suppose we all not merely could achieve most of the good things we aimed at, but we achieved all of them. Then almost everyone would be happy. In such a world we would all be aiming at the happiness of others because we would all be virtuous; and if we were achieving what we were aiming at, we would be achieving each other's happiness. If we were collectively virtuous, on this vision of the good, then we would collectively secure each other's happiness. It is true that even if everyone were virtuous, there could still be tidal waves and arthritis and severe depression. But even the victims of such natural evil would be embedded in loving relationships with other people and surrounded with compassionate and competent care givers. People engaged in the moral life at least have to believe in self-rewarding morality, that everyone's virtue would make almost everyone happy. We have seen how this belief is tied up with other beliefs they will have about themselves and about other people.

Moral Faith in Providence

However, belief in self-rewarding morality is not enough. Here is the turning point in the argument of this chapter. We have to be able to persevere in morality even if we do not believe that most other people are morally virtuous. We need belief in providence, the belief that the world is so ordered that a person's own virtue is reliably connected with her own happiness, *whether other people are virtuous or not*.

I do not know how high an estimate my readers will make of other people's virtue. My own estimate is not stable but varies with my mood and my most recent experience. Some days I get up and meet the people I usually meet, and they seem to me basically benevolent. Other days I meet the very same people, and they seem at best indifferent to my welfare and the welfare of others. I know there is very widespread gloom about the decline of virtue and decreasing trust (at least in the countries I know well) in the general goodwill of other people in ordinary circumstances. What is important for my present purposes, however, is not how virtuous other people actually are or even what the general belief is about most people's virtue. The important thing is that our commitment to morality does not depend upon our belief in the virtue of others.

Consider the fact that we try to teach our children to be moral. We also want them to be happy. If we thought that being virtuous would make them miserable, we would be more ambivalent about teaching them virtue than we actually are. But many people persevere in the attempt to bring up their children to be morally good people even though they do not think their children will live in a society in which most of their fellows are morally good people. If the idea of *self*-rewarding morality were the only kind of moral order we could believe in, this perseverance would be quite mysterious. What lies behind such perseverance is surely a belief that the world is so ordered that when their children grow up, they can be both morally good and happy, and that this is secured not by general human virtue but by something else.

The nature of this something else is often, I think, left indeterminate. My purpose at this point is just to get to this "something else." Eventually we need a more ambitious account of how this kind of moral order could have been achieved. I said earlier that moral faith in providence is faith in a moral ordering of the universe. The question we need to answer in the end is whether the ordering requires an orderer. We will explore that further in chapter eight. At this point I am just arguing that when we bring up our children to be morally good, we are committed to the belief that they will not have to do what is morally wrong in order to be happy; this belief does not depend on our believing that most other people are morally good.

What is the importance of the belief that the world is so ordered that it is possible for every person to be both morally good and happy? I think this possible state of the world functions for us as an ideal, and so inspires us to engage with the world as it actually is. But for it to function in this way as an ideal, we have to believe that this state of the world is possible. As I have described this ideal, it is extremely vague. Christianity has a more definite conception, the kingdom of God. This kingdom has the same character of being "already and not yet" as our righteousness (our being right with God), which I discussed in chapter three. We are already members of the kingdom and doing its work, but we do not yet see the kingdom in its full realization. The Hebrew Scriptures also have the idea that God promises a time when righteousness and peace (in Hebrew, *shalom*) kiss each other (Ps 85:10). The kingdom is a world in which we are all happy, but that is too flimsy a word if it means merely that we get what we want. In such a world we not merely have what we want, but what we want is what it is morally good to want. That is why it is *righteousness* and peace that kiss each other. Even the vaguer ideal I think we have is a vision that has the power to sustain us as we try to bring the actual world closer to the ideal than it now is. When we see glimpses of it, this vision allows us to hold them together into a pattern and to recognize them as significant. The possibility of the world being this way thus has a direct impact on our moral lives.

Moral Faith and Experience

I have said that we need this kind of moral faith if we are to persevere in the moral life. But it is also true that belief in providence is not clearly supported by experience. This is why moral *faith* is the right term here. Experience gives us all sorts of cases of morally bad people who are to all appearances happy (see Ps 73) and morally good people who are to all appearances unhappy. For example, we meet people who are trying as hard as they can to lead morally good lives but suffer from long-term severe depression. Our experience is thus consistent with a much bleaker picture of how the world is. Bernard Williams says the ancient Greek tragedian Sophocles represented human beings as dealing with a world that is vulnerable to the caprice of fate and which "is not necessarily well adjusted to ethical aspirations." Here is a competitor to moral faith and a much darker picture of our destiny. Actually, I think Williams is wrong about Sophocles. He is reading Nietzsche back into the ancient world because he finds Nietzsche's picture congenial. But I will not go into that here. He does present us with an alternative to moral faith, and that is what is important for now, not his historical judgment.

The same point of view can be found in all but one of the novels of Thomas Hardy and in much of the poetry of A. E. Housman, such as his poem "Terence, This Is Stupid Stuff":

> Therefore, since the world has still
> Much good, but much less good than ill,
> And while the sun and moon endure
> Luck's a chance but trouble's sure,
> I'd face it as a wise man would,
> And train for ill and not for good.

The sense of the world as tragic has a certain appeal. Camus, the French existentialist, tells the Greek myth about Sisyphus, a hero who was punished by the gods by being forced to roll a stone up a mountain again and again only to see it roll down again to the bottom. Camus imagines Sisyphus persevering in his pointless task but shaking his fist at the gods who require him to do it. The picture has nobility about it. Sisyphus does not pretend that his life makes any sense, but he perseveres by defying this absurdity. By contrast, it can seem that moral faith in providence is a bit weak-kneed or lily-livered. The faith that the universe fits our moral aspirations can seem a kind of self-gratifying fantasy, a failure to look harsh reality fully in the face. The evidence of the lack of fit between virtue and happiness in this life can seem overwhelming, so strong that only a fool or a bigot or a weakling would go on believing that the world is so ordered that we can trust that if we meet the moral demand we will be happy. According to this view moral faith in providence is not part of a truly admirable life.

Here it is relevant to look at the lives of those who have experienced great evil and have yet persevered in their faith in God. What do these lives show us? That experts in the experience of evil have not always found that this experience forces them to reject their faith. While I was writing my book *The Moral Gap*, I talked with a woman named Eva who was a survivor from the concentration camps of World War II. She said that her experience was that those who went into the camps with a strong faith in God came out, if they came out at all, with their faith stronger. They did not understand why God permitted the suffering, but their faith in God held them and kept them through it. Eva was Jewish, and I do not know whether she believed in an afterlife or not. My sense is that she did not. But she did have a basic attitude of trust that God was finally in charge and that the good was more fundamental in the world than the evil in it, and would in the end win.

A large biographical and autobiographical literature addresses this theme. Elie Wiesel, for example, who survived the camps as a boy, says that he has been angry with God and has not answered the question of why God allowed the Holocaust; yet he claims, especially in his later work, to have become closer to God through his wrestling and protest. Another survivor of the Nazi camps is Corrie Ten Boom, who saw her beloved sister die and almost died herself. *Lament for a Son*, by Nicholas Wolterstorff, deals with the death of his son. C. S. Lewis chronicles the death of his wife from a cruel disease in *A Grief Observed*. Joni Eareckson's *A Step Further* responds to a crippling injury to an athlete. Each of these people was forced by experience to be honest with God, but not to reject God. I am not discussing here the usual theoretical argument about whether the existence of evil is consistent with the existence of a good God. Rather, I am looking at the character of lives that contain moral faith even in the presence of overwhelming suffering. It is important that the lives of people like Eva are admirable. Their lives carry conviction. They have a reading of the enormous evil that they have experienced. They do not merely find the evil logically consistent with their faith (though that is important to argue). My point is, rather, that their lives are obviously praiseworthy, and it would be perverse to deny their goodness. Is there such a thing as a life of obvious goodness? Some would deny this. Christopher Hitchens, for example, wrote a book trying to debunk the myth of Mother Teresa. He has devoted his life to finding the worm in every bud. But I am content to rest on the claim that there is such a thing as an obviously good life even though not everyone will agree about every case; further, I want to claim that such lives will tend to be familiar with suffering and to display what I have called moral faith.

An instructive case is that of Ivan and Alyosha in Feodor Dostoyevsky's novel *The Brothers Karamazov*. Ivan tells the story of the Grand Inquisitor, which is often used in philosophy textbooks as the paradigm case of the argument against faith in providence. After telling a number of horrifying stories of evil, Ivan ends up saying to God that he respectfully returns the ticket (to the whole show). If this is the kind of world God is running, Ivan is saying, he wants no part of it. But we have to ask what Dostoyevsky is doing in putting this powerful section in the mouth of Ivan, with Alyosha as its audience. The philosophy textbooks take the passage out of its context and miss its point. What happens to these two brothers? Ivan, who does not fudge either the moral demand or his own radical incapacity, ends the book by going crazy and holding conversation with the devil. Alyosha ends the book declaring his faith to a group of children whom he loves and who love him. Dostoyevsky is trying to show us something. The story of the Grand Inquisitor is powerful, but it is not decisive. The life of Ivan, who is a man in the moral gap but without moral faith, is doomed; however, the life of Alyosha, who retains his faith without pretending that evil does not exist, is bound for glory. We can see in his life the character of the full kingdom of God toward which he is headed.

Thus morality requires moral faith in providence in the form of the belief that virtue is consistent with happiness whether other people as a general rule are virtuous or not. The next step is to ask what is the mechanism of providence. How is it supposed to work? All I have argued so far is that we need belief in something more than the virtue of other people. What could this "something more" be? Christianity brings in doctrines about God's work on our behalf, not just inside us but externally in the circumstances of our lives. I have not tried to prove these doctrines true; however, I have tried to show, so to speak, the space for them—where they are needed in a satisfying analysis of the moral life.

Providence and History

This chapter needs to answer one more question. What is the connection between providence, as I have defined it, and history? Chapter one claimed that morality as we are familiar with it has two components: a set of norms (and the values they support or express) and an organizing directive. These components have a background in

Christianity; the background to the organizing directive is especially the commandment to love the neighbor as the self. However, this background is not identical to the organizing directive; it is related to it by history. We have come to interpret the background in the light of the organizing directive over the last few hundred years.

There are two opposite errors we can fall into when thinking about this relation. The first error is to assume that the heart of morality as we are familiar with it has always been seen as morally central, and history has produced only peripheral differences. The second error is to think that morality as we are familiar with it is merely ours, as though we had been given it by a pure accident of history. This means thinking that morality as we are familiar with it has no special validity, even though we inevitably think morally the way we do, because of our historical context. I think the notion of providence gives us a way between these two errors, though it does not solve all the problems.

The first error of assimilating the whole history of morality to our own view is arrogant. It is blind to the fact that we have lost much that is morally valuable by the transition into the modern world. It is also blind to the value of much in the world that is not in our own tradition. I will try to give examples of both of these kinds of blindness, though I cannot pretend that my perception is free of the bias of my own cultural upbringing. Here is an example of the first kind. We inhabitants of the modern world have learned more about the independent value of women and children, but we have also lost a sense of the solidarity of the family. The same process has revealed something new to us and has hidden something old. It is good that people should not be trapped in abusive familial relationships, but when the option of breaking up a family becomes too easy, even good relationships become harder to maintain. I learned about the second kind of blindness when I lived in India and tried to practice contemplation. With rather limited success, I did nonetheless start to glimpse the possibility and the value of a more radical kind of emptying of the self than anything I had learned from Western culture. I think there is important truth here which is hard for a Westerner to grasp, though there are also dangers.

Saying that morality as we are familiar with it is *merely* ours is an error in the opposite direction, an error of too little confidence. It is true that we cannot justify our morality without already presupposing it. In the same way we cannot justify the basic principles of our science without presupposing them in the justification. But it does not follow from this that the principles of our science or our morality are merely cultural constructs. We may have seen something true, even though we cannot independently justify it. And there is some checking we can do. We can ask, first, whether a norm is part of the common stock of norms that seem to be present across cultures. Or the norm might be a version of one of those common norms that applies it to our particular circumstances, as, for example, the norm that requires unanimous verdicts in capital cases applies the common norm against killing the innocent. If so, we may have confidence that the common norm at least is not skewed by local preferences.

But suppose a norm is not merely a special application of a common norm but goes beyond the common stock. Human equality is such a norm. How then do we justify having confidence in it? One thing we can do is to see if there is any self-contradiction in it, or any convincing argument against it from other norms we endorse. Sometimes there will be a conflict between the traditional way of life where we live and some new norms that we are considering. In Homer, for example, there were norms of aristocratic excellence that confined virtue to those born in particular noble families. This did not fit the more democratic ideals that were already coming into Greece a century after the Homeric epics were first written down, and which started to extend the possibility of excellence outside the nobility. Somebody who lived at that time of transition could ask about the two rival pictures, "Does either one of them have more or better resources for explaining the other?" I think the case could have been made then (and indeed was made) that this new worth the ordinary folk felt had a validity the old ideals could not explain away and that attempts to deny it were in fact oppression.

Such arguments will always be tentative, however. In the end we have to have faith that if our norms pass the reflective tests I have mentioned, it is all right for us to live by them. I think this is a kind of faith in providence. It is a faith that living the way we have reflectively endorsed, if we have done the best job we can in this reflection, fits the way we are in fact supposed to live. This faith sees what I have called the organizing directive as a gift or call to us. It does not deny that the call comes to us through our particular history, since not all peoples at all times have heard it. But it locates the authority of this directive beyond history. This will strike those who do not believe the claim as arrogant. It looks like taking our central commitments and baptizing them in the name of God. This is what fanatics have continually done, and we need some response to this charge. The next five chapters of this book argue that we cannot find a good source for the authority of morality in the other alternatives that have been proposed. If this argument succeeds, and we do not have still further alternatives to propose, then we will be left with either God or denying that morality has authority at all.

What would it be like to take this second position, that morality has no authority? It would mean saying, "There is no particular reason why we should be moral. It's just a matter of taste. Some people feel drawn toward moral earnestness and others toward aesthetic pleasure and others toward making a lot of money. There is no more to be said. Of course, if you are drawn toward moral earnestness, you will think being morally good is the most important thing in the world. But that doesn't mean your preference has any special authority." Note that this is not the same as saying, "It is self-evident that we should be moral," which gives an answer to the question (an answer assessed in chapter six as insufficient). Rejecting the authority of morality is saying, rather, that there is *no* answer to the question, Why should we be moral? And this is not because the answer is obvious but because morality is genuinely optional. However, I do not see how the commitment to live morally can be sustained without the sense that it is based on something more than a person's preference or a person's taste for it. Perhaps this is merely because I am morally feebler than other people. But my experience of my fellow humans does not make me think I am unusual in this respect. The experience of the moral life is one of submission to something larger than oneself. We cannot take out that ingredient without radically changing the nature of the moral life. The question is what that "something larger" can be. The answers "human nature" or "reason" or "our community" are the topics of chapters seven, eight and nine.

We are left, then, with a situation similar to that described in terms of "already" and "not yet" in our discussion of the doctrine of justification in chapter three and of God's kingdom in this chapter. We receive the call to be morally good, and we have through our history interpreted it in various ways. The way we interpret it is fallible, and we can see in our history all sorts of abuses and blindness. But we have to believe that the way we have understood the call is "already" authoritative even though we do "not yet" understand the call in its completeness. The main topic of this chapter has been moral faith. This final section refers to what we might call "moral hope," the conviction that in the end we will see that the interpretation of this call that we have taken as binding on us fits how we were in fact supposed to live all along.

The first four chapters of the book compose the first of its two main parts. The question *How can we be morally good?* raised the problem of the moral gap. Chapter two mentioned three proposals for how we might deal with this problem without God. Chapter three described three Christian doctrines about how we might bridge the gap with God's assistance. The present chapter has suggested that people engaged in the moral life need to believe in providence, not merely for their inner transformation but for the external circumstances of human life. The second main part of the book will be about a different question, *Why should we be morally good?* The two questions are related: if we cannot be morally good, the question why we should be does not arise. Now that we've discussed the first question, we can go on to the second.

5

The Authority
of Morality

With this chapter the second main part of this book begins. The first part of the book asked whether we can be morally good without God's assistance. The second part of the book is about the authority of morality and whether we can explain it without God. Suppose I ask the question, Why should I be moral? I might be asking various different things. I might want to know, for example, why it is in my interest to be moral, or why being moral has a good chance of making me happy. These are important questions, and chapter four argued that we need to believe that morality is consistent with our happiness. However, if the discussion in the first section of that chapter was right, I can have sources of motivation other than my own advantage or my own happiness. I can have a love of what is good in itself, independently of my own happiness. Chapter one claimed that morality is concerned with the well-being of human beings seen as having equal and unique value. I can have a concern for this that is not dependent on its contribution to my happiness except insofar as I am one among all the others. So the question arises about how I should rank morality and my happiness. When I ask, "Why should I be moral?" I might be asking, "Why should I rank morality first?" Perhaps I am in a situation where morality requires something difficult from me, and this time I want a moral holiday. I want to let my happiness come first.

Rosa is taking a nap after coming home from a tiring day at school. She knows she ought to get up and prepare for tomorrow's class. There will only be time to do a good job if she starts right away. But it seems too hard, and the prospect of a bit more sleep seems too inviting. She does not deny that preparing the materials is what duty demands, but she asks herself, "Why do I always have to do my duty?"

Some philosophers have denied that this question makes sense. It will not make sense if a person's happiness is her only source of motivation, for then there cannot be the sort of ranking between morality and her happiness that the question implies. But even if we allow that she can be attracted to morality independently of her happiness, we might still have doubts about the question. What does she mean by "have to" when she asks, "Why do I always have to do my duty?" She might mean, "Why do I have to, if I want to be happy?" or "Why do I have to, if I want to be good?" But the first of these seems like a different question. She was asking why duty should come first even if it doesn't seem to be making her happy. And the second of these is puzzling. "Why do I have to do my duty if I want to be good?" is an odd question because doing her duty is part of what she means by being good. It's like asking why morality requires her to be moral.

We are going to examine five different answers that have been given to the question, Why should I be moral? This is not supposed to be a complete list of possible answers. But the fact that people have repeatedly tried to answer the question in these various ways suggests that the question at least makes sense. They are all proposals about what gives morality authority. One answer is that the authority

is obvious: we simply know intuitively that we are bound by morality, just as we intuitively trust the evidence of our senses. Another
answer is that we can deduce the authority of morality from human
nature: we can know that we should be moral by deduction from the
fact that we are human. A third answer bases the authority of morality on reason: any rational being is under the constraint of morality,
simply by being rational. A fourth alternative is to find the authority
of morality in community: our identity is formed by the community
we belong to, and we should be moral in order to be true to that formation. Finally, we might base the authority of morality in God's
will: something is obligatory for us if God commands us or calls us to
do it. We will look at each answer in turn, and I will argue that each
of the first four answers is insufficient. I will end by describing in
more detail the fifth answer, the divine command theory, or divine
call theory of moral obligation.

This chapter simply introduces these topics; it does not give a full
treatment of them. The next four chapters, however, take up the first
four answers in more detail, one to each chapter. They also do something else. They relate these four answers to four important things
"we" want to find in morality: transcendence, fulfillment, significance and a sense of belonging. Chapter six is about the idea that
goodness (including moral goodness) has an existence that transcends
us, pulling us as a magnet attracts iron. Chapter seven explores the
idea that morality fulfills human nature. Chapter eight discusses the
rational ideal for how our lives can be significant. Chapter nine
examines how community gives us a sense of belonging, but also
presents the dangers of relativism and exclusivity. These four chapters
argue that we will understand better the relation of morality to transcendence, fulfillment, significance and the sense of belonging if we
think of morality as the call of God. The final chapter discusses how
this call is related to our response. The present chapter is thus a kind
of introductory guide to the second part of the book as a whole, with

a section summarizing each of the succeeding chapters. The end of each section traces how the proposed answers to the authority question connect with the four things we want to find in morality.

Moral Perception

One suggestion is that the authority of morality is intuitively obvious, not requiring a proof. After all, proof has to end somewhere. This is a general point in philosophy. If you have to prove everything, you cannot prove anything. Somewhere you have to find a resting place in beliefs that serve as starting points without being themselves established by proof. Perhaps Rosa's belief that she should get up and prepare for class is one of these basic beliefs. A good analogy would be perception. If I see a goldfinch on a branch outside my window, I do not have to postpone believing that the bird is really there until this has been proved on the basis of something more fundamental than my original perception. The belief I adopt in the context of the original perception is as basic as it gets.

This does not mean that my perception-inspired belief is infallible. I might be the victim of a practical joke. Perhaps one of my neighbors (knowing me to be a philosopher who argues for the basic reliability of sense perception) has set up an elaborate apparatus involving a holograph in order to make me think there is a goldfinch there when there isn't. But in the absence of any special circumstances, like the deceitful neighbor or the rising hot air in the desert that produces an optical illusion of an oasis, I am justified in forming beliefs when I perceive something. Is the authority of morality like this? Is there moral goodness outside me that I sense or intuit, and if so, does this sense give me basic beliefs in the same way as sight or hearing?

Plato has a theory that posits a strong analogy between sensation and evaluation. He compares our experience of this world through sight to an intellectual "seeing" of the Forms, which are perfect versions of the imperfect material copies of them which we perceive down here. The Forms exist in their own perfect world, and they have an existence quite independent of us. They would continue to exist even if we all perished. For example, there is the perfect Form of Sphere and the perfect Form of Red, and we perceive round red things like billiard balls as roughly spherical and red because we have already seen the Forms intellectually. We see things here on earth as roughly good because we have already seen the Form of Good. Suppose Plato is right about how we see roundness and redness. Is he right also that we have a special kind of seeing we can do that has goodness rather than shape or color as its object?

The analogy is problematic. I have no memory of waking up in the morning with a general lack of faith in my capacities to see, hear, touch, taste and smell what is really there. I can imagine circumstances in which I would come to have this lack of faith; I might be a heavy user of hallucinogens, for example, or I might be coming back to consciousness after general anesthetic. But these are the same kinds of abnormal circumstance as the holograph and the optical illusion. On the other hand, the authority of morality is disputed on a regular basis. Rosa does not doubt that morality is telling her to get up and prepare the materials for class tomorrow, but she can always say to herself, "So much the worse for morality," and roll over and go back to sleep. In retrospect she may think this wrong and a sign of a weak character, but it does not seem *abnormal*.

People vary a great deal. Some people find that they cannot get to sleep if they cannot remember whether they brushed their teeth. Their sense of duty is so strong that it prevents them from doing what they know is in some sense more important, getting straight to sleep. On the other hand I am told that there are people who have no observable sense of right and wrong. Maybe there is a "seed of goodness" hidden deep inside them so that they can still hear the voice of the moral law or receive the signal that it transmits. But this voice is either completely ignored or has become so faint that it is more like an irritating memory of how they used to be than a present signal which they are receiving. Proper receptiveness in moral matters requires not just the receptors to be in good order but also the activity of the will.

This is true to a limited extent with sense perception as well. Often I have to choose to pay attention to something if I am going to see it or hear it properly. But once the eyes and ears are open and working properly, the will does not have to be actively involved in the reception of the information and the acknowledgement of its excellent claims to be believed. With the question of the authority of morality we are talking about a ranking that itself goes on in the will. When Rosa is in bed considering whether to get up, there is a competition going on in her will between the two motivations, roughly her happiness and her duty, with her will giving the final prize to one or the other. The notion of the will is a bit obscure here, and we will return to it in chapter six, which is about the relation, within moral judgment, between moral perception and decision. I will argue that when we make a moral judgment, we are endorsing in our will our initial prereflective response to a transcendent value that we perceive. I will explain the details of this view in that chapter.

For now, the important point is that granting authority to my perception of the goldfinch and granting authority to my perception that I should get out of bed are significantly different. It is a good answer to the question, "Why should I trust my senses?" to say, "Their authority is obvious." Perception is what the sense receptors are for, and in the absence of special circumstances it is simply unreasonable to doubt our present perception. But this does not seem like a good answer to the question, Why should I be moral? because moral response—for example, Rosa's judgment, "I should now do my duty and get out of bed"—requires not just the reception of signals from the moral law but choice, or reflective endorsement. Here doubts do arise, and the will needs to be given something to answer them. It is not enough to be told, "It's obvious."

Another way to put the difference between morality and sense-perception is to talk about the Christian doctrine of sin. Suppose there is a moral receptor in us called intuition, analogous to the sense-receptors (our eyes, ears, and so on). Actually I think this is an oversimplification, but that does not matter for now. The Christian doctrine of sin, according to one interpretation of it, holds that all human functions have been corrupted by the Fall, even sense-perception. But the effect of the Fall is not equally felt in all those functions. The effect is strongest in those functions closest to the will, since it was in the will that the choice to disobey God was made. So if we have a moral sense, or moral intuition, and if it is tied to the will in moral judgment in the way I claimed, we should expect sin to be more conspicuous here.

And indeed we do find this. The judgments we make about moral matters are much less trustworthy than our judgments about the visible or audible world. When I read in an ancient historian (like Xenophon) that after their long retreat the Greek troops finally saw the sea, I don't doubt that they did (unless I have a reason to think this particular historian unreliable). But suppose I read in an ancient moralist (like Aristotle) that the magnanimous person is justified when he thinks less of others, since his beliefs about his excellence and superiority are true even though most people are wrong if they think they are excellent; now I find myself suspecting that behind this view there is a static class system, which rewards its elite with wealth and honor. I don't trust the moral judgment here. The doctrine of sin explains this difference by saying that moral judgment is much more likely to be corrupt.

The sense that we are responding to transcendent values when we make moral judgments is correct, but the trouble is that our receptors are consistently defective. People routinely make monstrous errors in what they perceive to be good and confuse perception with self-gratifying fantasy. We need some kind of screening procedure to tell us when to endorse our perception of value and when to distrust it. One candidate for such a procedure is to ask whether our perception is consistent with what we know of the call of God. Other possibilities are to ask whether the perception fits our nature or is consistent with reason or conforms to the standards of our community. In any case, some such procedure seems to be required. Unlike the case of sense perception, it is not enough to say simply that our value perception is basically reliable.

Human Nature

A second suggestion is that we can deduce the authority of morality from human nature. Aristotle, born about fifty years after Plato, proposed that we could start by looking at what humans are naturally inclined toward or what they aim at in their conception of the good life. Then what is good will be what fulfills these inclinations or aims, since it will fulfill (or complete) our nature. If we are naturally inclined toward morality or aim at it, we can conclude that we should be moral in order to be human. "Be what you are" would be one way to put this. The slogan has an air of paradox about it; for if you are, let's say, blond, then you already are blond, and it does not make much sense to tell you to be blond unless we mean that you should change the color of your hair. But the term *human* is not quite like the term *blond*. The term *human* has a kind of direction already built into it. This is true of all biological species terms, as mentioned in the discussion of justification in chapter three. Suppose I see an acorn lying on the ground. It already has all the genetic information that entitles me to call it oak. But it is not fully or completely oak until it has sent down roots and grown into a tree; that is the direction in which it is headed. So for a human being the instruction "Be what you are" means "follow the direction given you by your nature." Chapter seven defends the claim that life is direction-pointing in this way. But I do not think this claim (even if it is true) gives us the right kind of answer to the question, Why should I be moral?

The problem is that the direction we are born with does not have the right kind of authority. Authority is a measure of right, not of power. I can be under the sway of another person or some internal addiction that has almost complete power over me but does not have authority to control my life. Might does not make right. We have to distinguish cases where power has authority and cases where it doesn't. Before making this distinction in the case of our natural inclinations, we have to ask what the natural inclinations are. This is difficult because there are rival notions of nature that are competing here. There is an important difference between what God created nature to be and what nature is after the Fall. It does not matter for the purposes of this chapter whether we say the Fall is an event at some time and place (the Garden of Eden) or a structure now of the whole created order but not a single event in time and place. The distinction between created and fallen nature will be the same in either case.

The same distinction can be made without referring to God or creation. The philosopher Immanuel Kant says that we human beings are born with both an initial predisposition toward good and, over the top of this, a propensity toward evil. This propensity means that the initial seed of goodness, the predisposition, cannot grow as it otherwise would into a good life. It is prevented by the propensity to evil, which makes us prefer or rank our happiness above our duty. So how should we describe our *natural* inclinations? We could stipulate that "nature" is to be confined to the predisposition to the good, and then it will indeed follow that the object of these inclinations is good. But the problem is that the nature we are born with is mixed; it contains both the predisposition and the propensity. We find ourselves moving toward both good and evil, and the tendency to put ourselves first is more powerful within our decision-making than the tendency to put first what is good in itself. This means that the inborn tendency has power over us, but does not have authority.

Aristotle's own ethical system is an excellent case study. He identifies as natural inclinations the pursuit of power and prestige. Since he thinks what humans are naturally inclined toward is the human good, his description of the chief human good includes power and prestige. He does not think most people get it, but it is what they almost all want. Only the completely virtuous man possesses the chief human good, he thinks, and complete virtue includes magnificence and magnanimity, both of which require wealth and high social status. But the trouble with Aristotle's view is that power and prestige are competitive goods in the sense that one person can have them only if other people do not (or at least have less of them). Leaders have to have followers, and social elites have to have the masses looking up to them. In the account in chapter one, morality requires thinking of all human beings as equally valuable. Chapter four expanded this requirement to include thinking that all human beings are capable of virtue. But this is inconsistent with thinking that most people are excluded from the chief human good. Aristotle is not wrong, I think, to say that we naturally pursue power and prestige; we do naturally pursue them. But Aristotle is wrong to think that it follows from our naturally pursuing them that they are good.

One key question is how to determine what we naturally pursue. Some contemporary forms of ethical theory claim to found ethics on an evolutionary view of human nature. We discussed some versions of this view in chapter two. They assume, like Aristotle, that the good is what we naturally pursue, and they assume, unlike Aristotle, that we can tell what our natural inclinations are by looking at the long hunter-gatherer stages of human history during which evolutionary pressure produced most of its effects. Thus Larry Arnhart, in *Darwinian Natural Right*, gives a list of our natural desires. The list includes desires for social status, for political rule (though this is, he says, a natural male desire, not a natural female desire), for war (again a male desire) and for wealth (that is, enough property to equip for a good life and to display social status). It is no surprise that when morality is deduced from this list, the moral demand is reduced. We will not need, for example, to love our enemies or to feed the hungry in the rest of the world. My conclusion about these theories is that the science is different from Aristotle, but the philosophical error is the same.

The sense that morality fulfills human nature is right, I think. But the problem lies in determining what human nature we are talking about. One possibility is the nature God created us with. If this is what we mean, then indeed we can say that God calls us to the kind of life that fits our nature like a glove. When we follow God's call, we flourish, and we can see how we have the equipment to live well with God's help. But if we mean the nature with which we are born, this is a mixture (as Kant says); what satisfies one part of the mixture may destroy the rest. So we need some test outside the nature we are born with to determine which part we should trust and which part we should resist.

Reason

A third suggestion is that we can base the authority of morality on reason. There are many different conceptions of reason, even within the history of Christianity. One version is Kant's. Kant wanted to base the authority of morality on something less limited than human nature. Reason, in his view, is possessed not only by humans but by God (and possibly finite intelligences other than humans, such as angels). Reason thinks universally, or thinks in terms of law. Thus in science we are not interested so much in whether some particular rock breaks some particular window pane when thrown with some velocity. The question is what law governs the impact of projectiles with a certain mass upon surfaces of a certain fragility. We do not think we have explained the particular event until we can subsume it under such a law. It is the same in morals, so the suggestion goes.

Reason is interested in the law governing whether people of a certain kind should act in a certain way in a certain kind of situation. If we consider such a law, we have to remove any reference to particular people or times or places. The law has to govern any situation that is similar in relevant respects. It has to be universal.

Rosa wants to park her car, but there is a bicycle in the middle of the last remaining parking spot. She considers moving the bicycle to the side in order to make room for her car, and (being a morally good person) she wants to check whether such an action is morally permissible. The present suggestion is that she can do this by asking herself whether she can will the proposal to move the bike as a universal law. This would mean willing it for any situation that was like hers in all the relevant respects. For example, it would mean willing it for the situation in which she was not the driver of the car, but the owner of the bicycle. Would she mind if someone who needed the parking spot moved her bike? In other words, she has to consider the proposal as if she did not know what role in the situation she was going to play, car driver or bicyclist. This is like the golden rule, which tells us (Mt 7:12), "In everything do to others what you would have them do to you." This instruction requires us to ask whether we would want something to be done to us if we had the preferences of the person being affected by our action (e.g., the bicyclist, if I am the motorist). But Kant's suggestion goes beyond the golden rule because it finds the authority of the requirement in the nature of reason itself, which always looks for the universal. If Rosa asks, "Why should I care whether my action is morally permissible or not?" the present suggestion is that the nature of her reason requires this. Her reason commands her to act consistently with what would be allowable universally, and not to make any special exemption for herself.

I want to mention two objections to this suggestion. These are not objections to the golden rule but to the proposed linkage with the nature of reason. Not all moral requirements are fully universal. I argue this in detail in chapter six of *The Moral Gap*. One way to make this point is to return to the claim in chapter one that morality values our uniqueness. Here Kant and Scotus diverge, and I think Scotus is right. For Scotus, what distinguishes humans from each other is more valuable than what we have in common. We have, as persons, individual essences, which are unique to us, and which are more perfect than the common essence that all humans share. If this is right and if reason deals only with what can be shared and not with the particular, then a central part of morality will be off-limits to reason. We will not be able to have moral relations that are tied to people's individual essences, since individual essences cannot be specified in a way that removes reference to the individual.

There is a conception of reason different from Kant's that allows moral obligations restricted to particular people to be rational. But if this is our conception, we will not be able to claim that reason is doing the same thing in morals and in science. Rosa reasons that she should help her daughter Lucy find her shoes because Lucy is in a panic. This judgment may commit Rosa to a similar judgment whenever Lucy is in this kind of trouble, but it does not commit her to a similar judgment about helping anyone else, even anyone else who is her daughter. In other words, reason (of this non-Kantian sort) can respect the uniqueness of persons and refuse to generalize from one person to another even though it generalizes from one situation to another affecting the same person.

There is another problem from the opposite side—not that reason is too restrictive but that it is not restrictive enough. A person can will to do something and be able to will it as a universal law that people should do that kind of thing, but it may still not be morally permissible. A fanatical Nazi had the ideal of a world without any Jews in it. He then found he had a Jewish grandmother, which was sufficient for being considered Jewish under Nazi law. He was able to be consistent about this and handed himself over to the authorities. But this does not mean that his genocidal ideal was morally permissible. To pass the universalizing test, he would also have to say that it is more important from the impartial point of view that there not be Jews than that all their preferences for life be respected. But surely even if he could say this, and say it sincerely, he would still be willing something morally wrong. Thus, the attempt to derive the authority of morality from the universalizing nature of reason fails.

We have a rational ideal of significance, of our lives making sense and being worthwhile. Kant is right that reason seeks to step back and to reflect. But *our* reason, the one we are born with and develop naturally, never reaches the position of the ideal observer who has all the relevant information and complete impartiality. We hope that our projects are coherent with the central values we share with those around us; that is a large part of what makes a life significant. But if chapter one was right about the organizing directive, the only person who could assure us of this would be someone who occupied the position described by this directive. Our reason indeed aspires to this position, but it is only God who has the authority to assure us that our lives do hang together and have value in this way. Moreover it is God who can see the unique nature of each of us and how our projects fit our own nature as well as fitting the projects and unique natures of others. A sense of significance requires confidence in a harmony of purposes that our reason is not in a position to provide. Chapter eight will expand on this point.

Community

A fourth suggestion is that we can find the authority of morality in community. Socrates, for example, proposed that we should think of our relation to our community (in his case, to Athens) in the same way we think of our relation to our parents. He did not know about genes, but he did know about heredity. We can put his point this way: "By their genes and by their nurture my parents have made me who I am, and my community forms me in the same way with its laws and customs. Morality is the glue that holds societies or communities together. I owe my community and its core values the kind of respect that comes from its having been a central part of my formation."

In a highly mobile society it is easy to lose this sense of loyalty. We imagine we can move anywhere and make new friends and new lives, selecting from pretty much the same range of restaurants and supermarkets wherever we go. What is so special about the place where we grew up? But the apparent similarity disguises how many possibilities have in fact been excluded and how much our lives are still borrowed from our upbringing. Visiting very different places and living in them can show us that many things we had assumed were inevitable are in fact optional. This fourth suggestion is that our communities have made us what we are, and the morality that is the core of the community therefore deserves our allegiance.

Hegel was a German philosopher about fifty years younger than Kant who bore a similar relation to Kant as Aristotle bore to Plato, being both deeply under his influence and also diverging in radical ways. Hegel claimed that Kant had not sufficiently valued the place of community in moral life, as Aristotle thought Plato had not sufficiently valued our material nature. The state, Hegel said, is not an aggregate of its citizens but an organism, and the citizens are members of this organic whole. A child is born into a whole life-world and does not even think of himself as separate. By the time he can separate himself from that world, his mind is already permeated with the language, the ideas and the practices of his community. If he turns against this, he turns against himself.

But there is a problem, which I will illustrate with an example. When I was growing up in England, my nanny told me that gentlemen polish the backs of their shoes. I knew that this was her way of instructing me to do the same. Ordinary people, she was saying, polish the fronts and sides of their shoes, but only gentlemen the backs. I remember also the college servant (called a "scout") who cleaned my rooms as an undergraduate saying to me sadly one morning, when my room was more than usually messy, "Sir, I thought you were a gentleman." I knew this was a very serious condemnation. But now I see that there is something wrong about a social system that divides a country into gentlemen (or ladies) and the rest. There were many admirable qualities associated with being a gentleman, but they were mixed up with class stratification in a way that I am now ashamed to have been part of. My question is what authority that way of life has over me now. I think it will always be important to me just because it was part of my formation, and I will never be able to eradicate its influence. Perhaps I will never be completely oblivious to the backs of people's shoes. But I can wish that I could be. The residual power of the idea is merely that: power. It is not authority. To get authority I would need some way, not itself restricted to that way of life, to distinguish what parts to reject and what parts to maintain.

There is another problem. Most readers of this book will belong to several communities at the same time, and even those communities will themselves be fractured to some degree. How are we supposed to tell which moral norms are constituting our identities? For example, I am now both an American and an Englishman, a philosopher in a particular department, a member of a particular congregation in a particular denomination, a resident in a particular neighborhood in a particular city, a citizen about to vote for a particular political party's candidate for president, and a member of a semi-professional choir and of several special interest groups. Each of these affiliations is itself to some degree divided between competing groupings. For example, some in the neighborhood want speed bumps and islands to delay traffic because they value safety and peace; and others want none of them because they value freedom of maneuver. So when I consider the various communities I belong to, I am faced with a battery of competing norms and values. How can mere membership give any of them authority when the resulting mixture is so incoherent? What we need is some way to sort out which memberships have authority and which do not. Hegel thought reason could provide such a test, but I doubt that his conception of reason can do this job successfully without begging the question. The moral screening proposed in the first chapter gives us a way to sort out when community deserves our allegiance. But then we still need to answer the question what gives *morality* its authority.

Socrates was right that we bear a relationship to our community like the relationship we bear to our parents. The sense of belonging to a community is a valuable gift that morality can give us because of its role as social glue. Perhaps people do have an initial responsibility of loyalty to their community and its standards, unless (like Athens with Socrates) it requires them to do something wrong. But the communities we are actually born into are a mixture, like the nature we are born into and our actual reason. In all these cases we do not get a source for the authority of morality unless we supplement them with something else.

God's Call

The fifth suggestion about the source of the authority of morality is that what makes something obligatory for us is that God commands it, or calls us to it. I prefer the language of "call" to that of "command" because I want to stress the love relation between God and us rather than the power relation. Rather than saying (as in the previous section) that I am created by my parents or by my community, this final suggestion is that I am created by God, and it is God's relation to me that gives morality its authority over me. Morality has authority because it is the route that God has chosen for me toward my ultimate end, which is union with God.

Suppose we ask, "Why did God create us?" According to the traditional Christian doctrine of creation, God did not have to create at all. God could have lived for eternity as the three persons of the Trinity in their mutual love for each other. There was no necessity binding God to bring into existence anything different from God. So why did God create us? We do not have access to God's mind on this question, and we should be diffident when we try to answer it. Nonetheless some answers have been proposed. I will mention a few and then offer one of my own, which relies on a distinction from Duns Scotus. Perhaps God created us just so as to be able to have other people to love. Or perhaps God created us in order to give expression to the divine love. Or perhaps God created us to increase the divine glory. The trouble with these ideas is that if we imagine a human having children for analogous reasons, they seem too self-serving. Such reasons no doubt motivate people to have children, but they do not seem to give the children the right kind of value. One response to this difficulty is to say that God is unlike us in this respect. Perhaps the notion of self-serving does not make sense when applied as an insult to God.

Another traditional answer is that God's love overflows all by itself into creation without any "ulterior" motive at all. Love is, we might say, inherently creative. But this view seems to make the creation too automatic, as though loving were under some force like gravity, inevitably pulling the lover toward the introduction of new entities and people. We need to preserve the idea of the freedom of God in creation, and it is hard for us to imagine any kind of freedom that does not involve motivation or purpose.

So here is another answer to add to the others: God created for the sake of what God created. The phrase "for the sake of" gives the purpose. But the phrase can be used in various ways, and it is useful to distinguish these, as Scotus did. I can pursue one thing for the sake of another where I see the first as a means to getting the second, like going to the dentist for the sake of future dental health. Or the first might be a constituent part of the second, like going to Timbuktu for the sake of adventure. But what I have in mind for understanding the creation is something different from either of these. I can do something for the sake of somebody where there is no self-reference involved. Rosa can help her daughter look for her shoes just for the sake of her daughter. This is an important feature of the account of motivation I took from Scotus, that we can be moved by the good in itself (and, he says, the good for another person) independently of its effect on our own happiness. I think God can be moved to create by love for what God creates, even though there is nothing there to love "before" the creation. If this is right, we can see creation as a kind of self-limitation, just as we limit ourselves when we love something other than ourselves for the sake of that other. God becomes vulnerable to disappointment by the very beings that motivated the creation.

This can help us understand how we image God in loving others. God creates us, I am suggesting, for our sake, and then wills for us a return to union with God from whom we came. Scotus says that our end is to be co-lovers with God, thus entering into the love between the persons of the Trinity. The route that God prescribes to this destination includes morality. The first chapter describes three features of the kind of screening that morality provides. We try to look from the perspective of the whole. We try to put an equal value on all people, not privileging ourselves. And we try to respect their uniqueness. We can now see how in all of these features we try to image or repeat God's activity toward us in creation and providence. God's view is the view of the whole, to which we only approximate very imperfectly. God creates all humans equally in the image of God. We try to value other people equally, and this has as its most difficult task loving the neighbor as the self. Here we image God's activity of self-limitation, loving another person for the sake of that other person. Finally, the uniqueness of each person is that individual's essence, the name written each on its own white stone as recorded in the book of Revelation. God's call to each person is to become that name; as Hopkins puts it in the poem quoted in chapter three, the task is to "selve." In honoring the uniqueness of others, we honor that call.

To sum this up, when we morally screen proposals for how to act or how to live, we are trying to repeat in our wills God's willing. One more qualification needs to be added, again from Scotus. The will we are trying to repeat is not exactly God's willing, because of the gap between us. It is God's willing for our willing, and that is what we hear as God's call.

6

Goodness

Chapter five made five suggestions about how morality gets its authority. The first of these was that the authority is obvious in the same way as the authority of sense perception. When I see a gold-finch perched on the tree outside my window, that perception has an authority that it is foolish to question unless there are special circumstances (like a malicious neighbor with a holograph). Do I have something like moral perception, which results in the moral judgment that, for example, my neighbor is malicious, or that Rosa is a good woman? And if so, does this moral perception have the same kind of authority as sense perception?

This chapter argues that there is a source of attraction and repulsion outside us to which we respond by valuing something as good or bad. But when we make a moral judgment, we do more than simply report such an attraction; we endorse it or refuse to endorse it. In my book *God's Call* I named this view "prescriptive realism." This view distinguishes various senses in which moral judgments can be objective. After arguing against the view that moral judgment is merely a projection of our preferences onto the world, I will suggest that when we make moral judgments we are trying to connect two centers, one inside us and one outside us. The inside center is the will, and the outside center is the quasi-magnetic center of attraction. When we make a moral judgment, we are trying to repeat the coherence of the outside center in the inside one.

It certainly feels as though we receive moral input from outside ourselves. We watch the bully on the school playground and feel both revulsion at his cruelty and compassion for his victims. We read about firefighters who climb up into a flaming skyscraper to rescue those who are trapped there, and we feel a mixture of admiration and awe at their courage. The cruelty of the bully and the courage of the rescuers seem part of the world outside us, prompting us to reject and admire. If we do not, that is a defect in us. In the same way, if we fail to see the goldfinch when we look out of the window, that is a defect in our vision. But as we began to see in chapter five, there is also a difference between these cases.

If we judge that the boy is a bully and that his cruelty deserves our contempt, we are not merely recording an impression from the outside, but we are also expressing our heart's response to it. There is both something outside here and something inside, both objectivity and subjectivity. The outside thing is what we are responding to, for example, the cruelty or the courage; it would be there whether we saw it or not. The inside thing is the heart's response that we are expressing in the judgment. Jesus says in the Sermon on the Mount, "Where your treasure is, there your heart will be also" (Mt 6:21). Our treasure is where we find value, and Jesus is saying that this is also the commitment of our hearts—our deepest loyalty. When we make a judgment of value, this is also an expression of our heart. The present chapter is about the relation between what is objective here and what is subjective.

Rosa's eighteen-year-old son Ned has a girlfriend, whom Rosa likes. But Rosa is conservative on the issue of sex outside marriage, and she is afraid that her son is going to start sleeping with his girlfriend before they get married. What does it mean to say she is afraid of this? It means that she construes it as a bad thing that might be about to happen, and this in turn implies that she is concerned about the sexual purity of her son. She cares about her son and she believes it is good for him to keep himself for the woman he eventually marries. The emotion of fear contains both of these features; she both construes the situation a certain way (as containing this bad possibility) and she has this concern or care. She construes the situation as dangerous because she loves her son, and the emotion takes up this love into how she sees what is happening. So the danger is outside her, and she feels inside herself a complex response to it. She may go on to judge that she should say something to her son about this. If so, she is endorsing her fear. We do not always endorse our emotions. Imagine a mother who is jittery about her son's chastity, but who has come to believe that there is really nothing wrong with premarital sexual activity. She considers her emotion an irrational hangover from her upbringing, and she rejects it. But this is not how it is with Rosa. When she watches the two of them together, she experiences this mixture of caring and construing that we call "fear," and she decides that this fear fits the situation. It is appropriate. And so she goes ahead and talks to her son about it.

Here is another example of this same three-part structure of outside pull, initial response and endorsement. I remember visiting the Cloisters in Manhattan, a museum of medieval art, and seeing a twelfth-century virgin and child, carved out of a single block of birch wood, the sole work of art in a small stone chapel. The figure of Mary was seated, holding the child on her lap. The wood was worn and cracked in several places, but the figure still conveyed a sense of regal strength and grief at what Mary knew was going to happen to her son. As I stood there, the light from a clear window fell on the statue and moved slowly over it until it crossed to the wall behind. I felt as though I was being given an extraordinary gift, which I could at any moment destroy. There was the beauty of the sculpture, and my emotional response to it holding me entranced. But there was also my gratitude both for the beauty and for my ability to see it. My will engaged with what I was feeling and affirmed it without reservation. Indeed, because I am a Christian, I understood the experience as God's pulling me like a magnet through the sculpture. *Pulling* is not quite the right word because it suggests that I was inert in the process, like an iron filing. I did have the power to turn away, out of embarrassment or nervousness or a refusal to concentrate any longer. But I also did not feel a mere invitation, in itself indifferent in value. Rather, I felt drawn by something supremely good beyond the sculpture itself.

We do not always experience all three parts of this structure. Sometimes the endorsement can be by default, like the default setting on a word processor that uses a certain font unless instructed otherwise. We do not always have to say "yes" to our initial response by a separate mental event of affirmation. Also the initial response to the outside pull is sometimes so familiar that there is no felt experience at all. But the model of these three parts gives the basic structure of evaluation.

Plato gives us a picture in the *Ion* of magnetic force and our freedom in response to it. He imagines a magnet with a whole chain of rings attached to it and compares it to a performance of Homer's poems. The muse inspires the poet, who inspires the performer, who moves the audience, and the magnetic force is transmitted by each ring to the ring below it. "Well, do you not see that the spectator is the last of the rings I spoke of, which receive their force from one another by virtue of the magnet? . . . But it is the deity who, through all the series, draws the spirit of men wherever he desires, transmitting the attractive force from one into another." But then Plato describes how the performer distances himself even at the moment of the transmission, "I look down upon them from the platform and see them at such moments crying and turning awestruck eyes upon me and yielding to the amazement of my tale. For I have to pay the closest attention to them; since if I set them crying, I shall laugh myself because of the money I take." We have this strange mixture of being drawn and yet choosing what to do about that response. In the case of the sculpture in the Cloisters I think God was drawing me toward union, and the sculpture was God's instrument. By affirming this experience as God's call to me, I was choosing to place myself under the authority of this call. I was endorsing the attraction.

Objectivity
We can distinguish three views about the kind of objectivity that is involved in valuing things. All three views are correct about different contexts. The first sees objectivity as impartiality in our valuation of a situation, the second sees it as the existence of values independently of our response, and the third sees it as an appropriate relation between what is really out there and how human beings respond to it by valuing.

The first view is the one associated with Kant in chapter five, that evaluation should be impartial. It should be objective in the way a good referee in a soccer game is objective. He is not swayed by favor for one team over the other even if one of them is his own team. All he wants to do is to apply the rules fairly. It does not matter which particular people are playing which particular roles in the situations he is evaluating. Anyone gets a yellow card who pushes another player from behind with the intent to get him off the ball. Morality is the same way. A plan of action I make for some situation is objectively permissible, under this view of morality, if I can will the plan universally for anybody in this kind of situation, not giving any special importance to the fact that I am playing a particular role in the situation. Chapter five gave the example of Rosa moving a bicycle in order to park her car. Subjectivity, by contrast, is the feeling of having an obligation, and it may or may not correspond to what the moral law in fact requires. Sometimes we feel that something is wrong or that something is morally permissible when in fact it isn't. For example, we can get used to a luxurious standard of living that is not consistent with sharing the legitimate purposes of people in the developing world. We get morally lazy, and the divide between the rich and the poor stops bothering us. Our goal, in this scenario, should be to bring subjectivity and objectivity together so that we feel we have an obligation when we in fact have an obligation, and there is no gap between them.

A different view about objectivity is the one associated with Plato in chapter five. Plato believed in Forms, like the Form of the Good or the Form of the Beautiful, that exist in their own world. He thought it was these Forms that had objectivity in the true sense. They are, he said, the only things that are "really real." They have an existence quite independent of us and would continue to exist even if we all perished. We are drawn toward them by a kind of love, which starts with loving the material things that imitate the Forms and then is led by upward stages toward loving the Forms themselves. When we do "see" the Form of the Good, we are caused to desire to make the world more like the Form, that is to say, better. This kind of objectivity differs from the preceding one because it appeals to entities which exist independently of us, whereas the previous kind of objectivity derived from a procedure that we engage in, namely willing a plan of action universally. Our subjective state, for Plato, is our response to the Forms, and here (as in Kant) we have the task of getting our response to fit more adequately with what is objectively true.

In several of the dialogues Plato describes how Socrates asks a series of questions to his conversational partner, often starting with material examples that copy the Form. Sometimes the interlocutor "sees" the Form suddenly, under the pressure of these questions. In Plato's view what he "sees" is something he is in fact recollecting from a previous experience of the Forms before he was born into the body he now occupies, so he has the "aha!" experience of recognizing what in a sense he already knew but had temporarily forgotten.

A third view of objectivity comes from reconsidering the analogy with visual perception. When I see something red, like a tulip, I might wonder whether the redness that I see is in me (in my sensation) or in the tulip. But perhaps the truth is neither of these. Perhaps the redness is a tendency in the tulip to make people see "red" when they look at it, if their eyes are working properly and the tulip is in good light. If this is right, the redness is not exactly in the tulip or in me but in the relation between us. If we know enough of the physics and biology of the situation, we can give a partial account of this natural tendency in terms of the object reflecting a certain wave-length of light and the rods and cones of my eye receiving it. We will also need to refer to what the experience of seeing red is like from the inside. The important thing for present purposes is to realize that both these things are necessary, the right condition in the object and in the perceiver. When I judge that the tulip is red, I am claiming that these conditions are in fact right and that I am not being misled (by a malicious neighbor, for example).

Moral goodness is like this as well. When we read about actions like the firefighters' going up into the flaming skyscraper, we have the tendency (if our moral faculties are working properly) to feel admiration. There is a quasi-magnetic pull on our emotions. This pull is exercised on us from outside, but it cannot be understood without reference to our responsiveness under proper conditions. When I judge that the firefighters' action is morally good, I am claiming that this pull toward admiration is legitimate; it fits the facts. The proper conditions, I claim, are being met both by the object (the firefighters' action) and the subject (myself, the moral evaluator). I am here endorsing the emotion I feel, like Rosa endorsing the fear she feels for her son. So the truth of the judgment is both objective (being about the object) and subjective (being about the subject), and the judgment can go wrong on either end (the object may not merit this response in me, and my reception may be defective).

There is truth in all three of these pictures in different contexts. Impartiality is indeed a virtue in a referee and in most of moral life. This is the first kind of objectivity. God is objectively real in the second way, the way Plato thought the Forms were real. In other words, God's existence is not relative to our capacities to apprehend God. But values like courage are objective in the third way. They are to be understood in terms of how we should respond to them. Courage is distinguished from foolhardiness, for example, because it is the kind of risk taking we should admire. There is a circle of evaluation here, in which the value is to be understood in terms of our appropriate response, and the appropriate response is to be understood in terms of the value.

The quasi-magnetic pull from outside us may have many different characters. A magnet also repels, and some things we encounter can repel us. Rosa sees the bully on the school playground and hates his cruelty. But even attraction can have many different forms. It is a mistake to look for just one feature that we always experience when we feel pulled toward something good. The experience of hearing a good joke is quite different from the experience of riding a good mountain bike or going to a good performance of Beethoven's *Fifth Symphony*. But while these are different, we hope for a certain kind of coherence between them. We hope that there is a magnetic center that holds all these pulls together and unifies them. That is a role Plato gave to the Form of the Good, which he thought made all the other Forms intelligible. In the final section of this chapter we will return to this idea of a magnetic center in connection with the ideas of God's call and our endorsement.

Projection

This analysis of valuing distinguishes three components: the quasi-magnetic pull from outside, the emotional response to that pull and the endorsement of that response in the value judgment. We can now discuss the error of philosophers who ignore the first of these components. They think of moral evaluation as a kind of projection onto the world. Before discussing the error, I want to concede that we often do project our desires onto the world. The question is whether that is always what we do when we evaluate.

Despina is the very opposite of Rosa in moral character. She despises the poor and sees them as loathsome, groveling creatures who are either out to trap her into pity and charitable donation or else to attack her if she lets down her guard. When asked to justify her contempt, she says that she sees them as they are, because unlike most of us she does not filter her perception through conventional pieties about compassion and human dignity. She is merely responding, she says, to the disgusting mixture of obsequiousness and hostility that she sees around her. And when she reflects about her response, she finds that she can endorse it wholeheartedly. She has a whole moral, political and economic theory about self-reliance and the survival of the fittest which she claims validates her response and embeds it in a rich context of explanation. We might think that all she is doing is projecting her own ideology onto the people she meets, so that she takes her experience to confirm her views, whereas actually it is the other way round: her views are coloring and forming her experience. But she thinks just the same about us and all our formulas about the inherent dignity of persons. The hard question is whether we have a stalemate here, or whether we can make progress toward understanding when values are in fact there outside us and when they are not.

The philosophers whose views I want to attack in this section say that evaluation is always projection. They insist on imposing a certain dichotomy. Values are either outside us, they say, in the way armadillos are outside us (things we discover) or they are things we put into the world, like armchairs (things we create). They then deny that values can be in the world independently of us because of the obvious link between valuation and our desires, emotions and will, which are obviously inside us. They conclude that values must be our creation or our projection onto the world. There is a good deal of technical philosophy involved, which I will try to summarize. The essential point is that the dichotomy itself—either discovered or created—is a mistake.

Rosa makes the value judgment that the behavior she saw on the school playground was wrong. This brings into play all three components I previously described. She is endorsing the initial revulsion she felt in response to something repugnant in the world outside her. To express endorsement is not merely to report something, but to express a commitment of the will. This is a subtle but important point. We tend to think that language always works the same way, to make reports either of what is out there in the world or inside ourselves. But much of language does not have the function of making reports at all. If I sit on a pin and say, "Ouch," I am not reporting that I have pain but expressing my pain. Rosa says to her daughter, "Go and look for your shoes in the bathroom." She is not reporting anything but giving her daughter a command, which expresses (but does not report) her desire that her daughter go to the bathroom to look for the shoes.

Sometimes our language marks these different functions with different grammatical forms. For example, "Go" is imperative and gives an order, unlike "She goes," which makes an assertion, or "Is she going?" which asks a question. Sometimes, however, there is no grammatical marker that indicates that something other than mere reporting is going on. "What he did was wrong" is a case in point. The sentence looks at first sight as though it is just an assertion, like "She goes." But we can see that it is not a mere assertion if we reflect on how odd it would be if Rosa said this, and then when she was offered a chance to stop the bullying without any harmful side effects to her or anyone else she refused to do anything about it. If she did this, I think we would doubt the sincerity of her initial judgment. We would think that she didn't really mean it. This shows that when she says to us, "What he did was wrong," it has another function besides merely reporting to us the existence of something (the wrongness) outside her. We should take her as expressing her will to stop the bullying if she gets the opportunity. This is why the dichotomy—values are either discovered or created—is a mistake. Value judgment involves finding something (a value) in the world, but that is only part of the story. There is also the expression of the will.

It is consistent to say both that there is some force from the world outside that Rosa is responding to and that she then endorses that response in her judgment. Our experience is not deceiving us here; there really is this kind of force. The image of magnetic pull is appropriate here, and it is hard to find a more literal way to put it. Things we see and hear move us. But we still need some way to sort out when things *deserve* to attract us or repel us. We have the freedom to choose what to do with our response, as Plato described the performer of Homer's poems distancing himself from the grief he was transmitting to his audience. We need to be able to distinguish Rosa from Despina, who finds the weak disgusting. We want to say that Rosa is responding to a value that is really there, but Despina is merely projecting value onto the world from her own ideology. How can we justify this distinction? We are trying to sort this out when we deliberate about whether or not to endorse our initial response. We need a normative theory in order to do this or a set of standards to apply. This is the topic of the final two sections of this chapter.

The Inside Center

Rosa is late for work, and she is angry with her daughter Lucy for losing her shoes. When she snaps at her and Lucy bursts into tears, Rosa realizes that she has overreacted because of the time pressure. She says she is sorry, and they both go looking for the shoes together. Here we have a complex example of the three components of evaluation under discussion. We can now focus on the third of these, namely endorsement. In the throes of Rosa's anger she construes her daughter as negligent and careless and insensitive to her mother's need to be on time. The rebuke she gives her is meant as a kind of punishment for these failures, and she intends it to hurt and sting. That is part of being angry. But when Lucy dissolves, Rosa's anger dissolves as well. It is still true that her daughter has misplaced her shoes, but Rosa now remembers how often she used to do the same thing when she was her daughter's age. She remembers thinking that her shoes had a will of their own and walked about the house just to spite her. She comes to see that her anger was inappropriate, caused by her getting flustered by the time constraint (which often happens to her), and she now refuses to endorse her initial reaction.

What justifies her in this refusal? Basically, she comes to see two things: the anger was not really her, her true self, and it did not fit who her daughter really is. She knows that she is not really an angry person (though she sometimes gets angry, just like everyone else), and that Lucy is not really a thoughtless person (though she sometimes acts thoughtlessly). In Romans 7, according to one interpretation of this difficult passage, Paul talks about inner conflict in these terms, "For I do not do what I want, but I do the very thing I hate. Now if I do what I do not want, I agree that the law is good. But in fact it is no longer I that do it, but sin that dwells in me" (vv. 15-17). Paul agrees that some act he does is wrong, but he says there is something inside him, which he calls "sin," which leads him to do that very act. It is no longer he that does it. We often experience ourselves desiring or doing something that is not really us. One kind of case is where the desire seems like an alien intruder coming out of nowhere.

Weird and bizarre ideas can suddenly pop into our heads. I pass an old man on the street, leaning heavily on his cane, and to my horror I suddenly imagine kicking away his cane, causing him to fall helplessly to the ground. I will not in fact do such a thing, but for a moment I contemplate doing it. Or sometimes we have desires that we acknowledge as familiar enemies, which we have been struggling against for years, like an alcoholic's desire for a beer. Or our desires can be not enemies but more like a loyal opposition, the other side of desires we value highly.

Tom is very good at concentrating on his academic work. The other side of this is that he is hopelessly bad at looking after young children when he is trying to read at the same time. He can totally ignore crashes and yells from upstairs that would have Rosa up there in a second. This desire for focus can be both good and bad, depending on the situation. When Tom finally smells smoke, rushes up to the room, and sees Lucy trying to put out a fire on her rug with her bed sheets, he wishes that he had not been so absorbed in his reading. That focus was indeed him, but not the way he would prefer to use who he is.

Desires may not fit who a person is for various reasons. I will start with the most extraneous, where it is easiest to see that the desire is not me. Perhaps I have been hypnotized so that whenever I smell pizza I have the urge to stand up and sing the national anthem. Suppose then I am in church listening to the sermon, and I smell pizza from the kitchen where the youth group is preparing lunch. I suddenly feel a strong urge to jump to my feet and sing, "Oh say can you see . . ." I will experience this desire as an alien intruder. But our minds can play the same tricks on us as a hypnotist, introducing foreign ideas beyond our conscious control.

Or someone may suffer from a condition like kleptomania, and the desire to take a shiny golden pen set from the shelf of a store may suddenly overtake her irresistibly as she walks past it in the aisle. In some sense the desire is not her, though the condition is hers. Or someone may have a personality disorder as a result of which he thinks he is Napoleon. He combs his hair the same way and speaks in late-eighteenth-century French. He thinks ceaselessly about strategies to revenge himself on Wellington. But these desires are, in some sense difficult to define, not authentically his own. Finally, someone may have been severely and continually abused as a child, and it may become impossible for him to form loving relationships with other people. He simply does not have enough trust, and the desire to keep his distance is overwhelming. But I think there is still a sense (but now only barely) in which this is not him. Perhaps all that is left is a sense that there is something important missing from his life, which he does not have the words for.

How are we to make sense of these cases? I think that we have the idea of an integrated center in a person, and that desires only count as fully authentic if they come out of or are consistent with this center. I am calling this center "the will," but another term might be "the heart." Some philosophers think that the idea of the will is hopelessly confused, or that there is no such thing. But we certainly have the experience of endorsing our desires as if from such a center. I think the objection to the idea of the will comes from two sources.

One point is that we are not always conscious of a separate act of the will whenever we endorse something. As stated earlier, sometimes endorsement can be a default position. The computer on which I am currently typing has a default font setting of Times New Roman. It will set me up with Times New Roman unless I tell it not to, and I do not have to make a separate decision each time. In the same way, if a person's desire is consistent with his or her central commitments, it can be endorsed by default even though there is no separate act of the will to endorse it. Still, the normal case of endorsing involves the will, whether by a separate act or not.

The other source of doubt about the will is that some people do not seem to have a "center" at all. Centrality comes in degrees. Often a fifty-year-old will have more integration of her desires than an adolescent. Because she knows herself better, she will know when her core commitments are at stake in getting some particular thing she wants, and when there are alternative routes to this core and the particular thing is negotiable. Intensity attaches to an adolescent's desires less selectively. So the ability to endorse a desire from a personal center also comes in degrees. We do not hold an eight-year-old fully accountable for killing someone, partly because at the age of eight a person has not yet matured enough to make full endorsement possible. Still, for normal adults we make this kind of distinction between core and periphery.

In all the cases described earlier, the person's will has been bypassed, or perhaps in the cases of personality disorder or severe abuse there is no will to be bypassed. This is not to say that only virtuous desires can be endorsed by a person's will. But a desire is not willed unless it comes through or is at least consistent with this personal center. The hypnotically induced desire to stand up and sing the national anthem fails this test, and so does the desire to kick away the old man's cane. So does the desire to steal the pen set and the alcoholic's desire for a beer. The desire by "Napoleon" to revenge himself on Wellington is harder; but if he has a personality disorder, he may not have the kind of integration that our notion of will requires. It may be possible for people to lose, either by mental illness or by bad life-choices or by victimization, any sense of coherence in what they centrally desire for themselves. People who were abused as children will have lost this kind of integration if they cannot recognize in themselves the remnants or fragments of the desire for sustained relationships and if they do not even realize that they do not trust people enough to try.

The Outside Center

Endorsement requires this kind of personal center, but it also requires a center of another kind, what I earlier called a "magnetic" center. This is a center of attraction outside the person, which she thinks of as holding together the various things toward which she finds herself drawn. Plato gave this role to the Form of the Good; but he also used the image of the deity exerting quasi-magnetic force through one iron ring to another, with the individual human being at the end of the chain of rings.

The Christian tradition has given this role to God. Christians can believe that the good things drawing them are all parts of the route toward their union with God. The birch-wood statue of the virgin and child, for example, and the firefighters' acts of courage, and the ideal of keeping sex within marriage, and the pleasure in riding a well-engineered mountain bike on a beautiful woodland trail—all these things hold together in a coherent whole, because they are signals from a single source. They can compete with each other in the sense that a person can be drawn toward different good things at the same time. For example, she cannot at the same time contemplate the statue and ride the bike. But they are all intrinsically endorsement-worthy, though not as proposals for simultaneous action. If the believer endorses one of these attractions as a proposal for *action,* she can believe it is consistent with the other attractions she proposes to act on. She can believe these proposals fit together because they are all parts of God's plan for her. God has called us toward various good things for us to do, "good works, which God prepared in advance for us to do" (Eph 2:10). Our task is to discern the right order of these good things, and one way we do this is the moral screening described in chapter one.

Imagine what would happen if we did not have this sense of coherence. Suppose we believed there was a malignant demon in charge of the world who took pleasure in making us do harm to people whenever we tried to do them good. I mentioned this thought experiment in chapter four. The philosopher Descartes imagines something like this in his *Meditations,* except that he pictures the demon as making us believe something false whenever we try to believe something true. But suppose the demon was interested in mucking up our pursuit of what is good rather than our pursuit of what is true. I think we would stop trying to do good. There would be no point in it. We have to believe that the good things we try to achieve in action can be reached together as a coherent set. We have to believe, in other words, that there is no such demon or that such a demon does not have final control of the world. Moreover, if we care about other people (as morality requires), we have to believe that our proposals cohere with their good proposals for action.

There is a massive coordination problem here in seeing how all this coherence could be sustained. We will return to this in chapter eight. For now, I want to point to the need for an external center of attraction in addition to the internal center, which I called the will or the heart. For a Christian, endorsement works like this: it is an attempt to discern whether the particular attraction that she feels toward something is consistent with God's will, and then to repeat God's will in her own will. For someone who does not believe in God, there is still the need for an analogous way to do endorsement. The unbeliever will need a way to check whether the attraction she feels is consistent with the good as a whole, and so whether the thing attracting her deserves to attract her or whether her positive response to it is somehow out of order. Chapter one used the analogy of a good driver who needs to check the rear-view mirror. The organizing directive is a way to test whether acting on some attraction is morally permissible.

We probably cannot see very clearly either of these two centers, the one inside or the one outside. Plato puts the difficulty with seeing the outside center in terms of his picture of the sun, which stands for the Form of the Good. If we try to look at the sun directly, we will merely be blinded; but the sun is nonetheless the source by which we see everything else. In Christian terms, we do not have access to God's will, except as God chooses to reveal it to us; and the revelation is never going to be more than a glimpse. The inside center is also hard to see. We are easily deceived into a good opinion about ourselves; but, paradoxically, we can flip in a moment into thinking of ourselves as mere worms, beneath contempt. We never see clearly and definitively into our own hearts, though a Christian thinks God can see us as we are and judge us accordingly.

Despite these difficulties, endorsement is the attempt to connect these two centers. It is the attempt to bring our responses to what we feel is good under the discipline of our commitments as a whole (integrated by the internal center); this means that our commitments have to be part of the route that will in fact take us to our good and to the good of everyone else as a whole (integrated by the external center). We are trying to make our commitments like the rings held together by the magnet. Even though we cannot see either center clearly, we have to believe that we can repeat at least partially the coherence of the outside center in the decisions we make inside.

We can end with the example of Rosa and her daughter Lucy. When her daughter dissolves into tears, Rosa feels the call from the relationship between them back toward reconciliation. She realizes that she has damaged a relationship she cares a lot about; by saying she is sorry and going with her daughter to find the shoes, she takes the steps toward restoration. She also hears in this call of the relationship the call of God. What does this add? Her experience is both like and unlike seeing the sculpture in the Cloisters as described at the beginning of this chapter. The difference is that she is prompted by something missing, not something present. She feels a sense of distance from her daughter and a sense that this distance is incongruous or false to the nature of their relationship. The call is not to stay where she is and enjoy the experience, but to repair a breach she has made. The similarity between the experiences is that there is in both cases the pull from something beyond the immediate context.

In Rosa's case, when she says yes to what she feels, she links up this sense of call with her commitments as a whole and the source of their authority. This relationship with her daughter is one that God has blessed, and Rosa believes God will continue to bless it. She believes she has been given her daughter as a gift and that she is accountable to God for what happens to her. She has beliefs about God's patience with us when we constantly fail to live as we should, and she wants to repeat this kind of patience in her own life. She remembers the passage from Colossians where we are told to get rid of anger because you "have put on the new self, which is being renewed in knowledge in the image of its Creator" (3:10 NIV). Rosa believes that if she restores this relationship with Lucy according to the model of how God restores relations with us, this can contribute to a world that is good for everyone, herself and her daughter and everyone else whose life is affected by the two of them. In a word, her action can contribute to God's kingdom. The relationship does indeed have quasi-magnetic force on her, but she endorses that or grants it authority when she relates it in this kind of way to the kingdom as a whole.

This chapter has discussed the analogy between moral sense and perception. We do receive moral input from outside ourselves, just as we receive sensory input in perception. But the process of endorsement is different in the moral case, and we need a way to connect the input with our commitments as a whole. A person who believes in God will see God as the center who keeps these commitments coherent. This chapter has not argued that only God can play this role. It has argued, however, that merely feeling an attraction or a repulsion from something outside us is not enough to provide authority. The authority is not in that sense self-evident. Despina just as much as Rosa has such feelings and has moreover an elaborate ideology by which to evaluate them. If we are going to say that Rosa's moral sense is authoritative and Despina's is not, we need to say why. We have to appeal to something beyond the fact of being attracted or repelled and having some larger story to tell. The moral screening discussed in chapter one provides an account. But if so, then the sense of attraction from outside cannot be the source of the authority of morality; the relation is the other way around. Moral screening allows us to endorse the sense of being attracted to something and to grant it authority. But then mere attraction cannot be the source of the authority of morality, and we need to find this source in the way this attraction is connected to the outside center that holds together the things that draw us.

7

Human Nature

Chapter six described Plato's view about the Forms, which he thinks are the only things that are "really real." The question of the chapter was whether we can derive the authority of morality from our attraction to something that transcends us, in the way the Forms transcend us. The answer was that we need moral screening to determine when we can treat such attraction as authoritative and when not. Aristotle's view of what is real is very different from Plato's. He did not think that a separate world of the Forms was helpful in understanding the world in which we live. The most basic kind of reality for him is what he calls "substance." The present chapter examines whether we can get an account of the source of the authority of morality from an Aristotelian view of substance, and in particular an Aristotelian view of human substance.

The distinction between the two philosophers is displayed vividly in a fresco that Raphael painted in the Vatican in the sixteenth century. Since the eighteenth century the fresco has been called "The

School of Athens." It depicts a gathering of the great thinkers of classical antiquity arranged in small groups which in turn make up a large circle, like the circle of the stars in classical astronomy. They are placed in a magnificent domed Renaissance church or temple, which is open at the back to the blue sky beyond. The focus of the painting is on Plato and Aristotle. Plato is an old man with long white hair and beard, and Aristotle (who was Plato's student for twenty years) is young, with his brown hair and beard trimmed. Each is holding in his left hand a book he wrote, Plato the *Timaeus* (which describes the causal influence of the eternal Forms) and Aristotle the *Nicomachean Ethics* (which describes the best life here on earth for human beings). With the index finger of his right hand Plato is pointing up to heaven, and his arm and the book he holds are both vertical. Aristotle spreads out his right hand, gesturing down toward the earth, and his arm and the book he holds are both horizontal.

Raphael is giving us a view not just of the two men but of their philosophies. For Plato the Forms are *beyond* us; our eternal souls get glimpses of them in our bodily lives through disciplined contemplation. For Aristotle the Forms are *in* the substances we experience; our task is to make sense of this experience, not to move beyond it. There is one more thing Raphael is doing in this fresco. By the way he has set up the figures he is suggesting that Plato and Aristotle, while in dispute, are both a necessary part of the whole truth. It is as though they are together generating the forces (upward and inward) that keep the whole circle of thinkers rotating in their prescribed orbits.

The next section describes an Aristotelian view of substance. In the third section we will discuss how that view has been used to make what I think is an error, the attempt to deduce our moral obligations from an account of human nature. The fourth section claims that the moral law is God's choice, not required by human nature. The final section supports the view that morality fits human nature exceedingly well, even though it cannot be deduced from it. I will defend the claim that we flourish when we keep the moral law, and we deteriorate when we break it. This is indeed a connection between morality and fulfillment. But it does not make human nature the source of the authority of morality. The source is God's choosing to give beings with our nature this route to a loving union with the divine nature.

Substance

Aristotle views Forms as being in substances; he thinks of substance as the fundamental kind of being on which all other kinds of being depend. Rosa is a substance. When she gets a tan on her summer holiday, the existence of her tan depends on the existence of Rosa, and Rosa's existence does not depend on the existence of her tan. Aristotle's account stresses the role of substance as the cause that underlies and explains change, and he describes two fundamental kinds of causation: matter and form. Form is the internal organizing activity of a thing, which gives that thing unity through change. Matter is what form organizes. This account does not, however, split a substance into two different things, in the way Plato splits up animals into body and soul, which can be separated at death. For Aristotle, a substance is not two different things joined together but an inseparable unity.

For Aristotle the form-matter analysis goes through a number of different levels. If we consider a living substance, say an armadillo, we can analyze it into its form and its matter. Its form is its characteristic armadillo-type activity, and Aristotle says its soul is its capacity for this activity. Its matter is the flesh and bones that are organized in this activity. We can then take, say, the bones, and see that each bone can be analyzed into bony stuff (the matter) and its organization for doing the kind of things a bone does (the form). And the bony stuff can in turn be analyzed into some more primitive stuff and its arrangement and activity. The process of development is the reverse of this process of analysis, and can best be understood as a direction toward form. The more primitive kinds of matter are changed from simple to compound (e.g., from inorganic to organic) by the imposition of form at different stages until we have something that is ready to be a mature armadillo. When this happens, the matter has been all used up, so to speak. There is nothing left for it to become in the direction of substance. There is still potential for change (the armadillo can roll up in the face of an enemy, such as a car). But the only remaining change in *substance* is regressive. The armadillo can decay, when it is killed, into flesh and bones, and the bones into bony stuff, and eventually into inorganic stuff, ready for the process to begin all over again.

Aristotle's point, as I understand it, is that only living things have the right kind of self-directed development to count as complex substances in this sense. A heap of sand is not a substance. If we take the various grains of sand that make up the heap, they can be in contact with each other. But they do not make up the kind of unity that persists through change in the way science is looking for. The same is true if we take the drops of water that make up a lake, or the clods of earth that make up a field. This is also true of human artifacts. A ball bearing and a baseball do not have the right kind of unity through change, because the principle of their persistence is not in themselves but in their makers who designed them for some purpose. Because the baseball has a different purpose from the ball bearing, it does not have to be so perfectly spherical. Its purpose and its shape are not given by an internal source of change and development but by the people who make it.

Aristotle's view of substance is essentially biological and has been confirmed to a surprising degree by contemporary science. His view does not depend on his physics and chemistry, which are outdated. A current biologist, J. Z. Young, supports Aristotle's view as follows: "The essence of a living thing is that it consists of atoms of the ordinary chemical elements we have listed, caught up into the living system and made part of it for a while. The living activity takes them up and organizes them in its characteristic way. The life of a man consists essentially in the activity he imposes upon that stuff."

This account of substance does not reduce the importance of matter in the style of Plato's *Timaeus,* which teaches that material things are defective copies of Forms in another world. On the other hand it does not reduce the importance of form by teaching that everything is matter and that we can in principle reduce psychology to biology, and biology to chemistry, and chemistry to physics. If we accept Aristotle's account of substance, at least in outline, what implications does it have for our account of value? Life is, in the account outlined here, a directional idea. To be alive is to be able to cause changes (both internal and external) in the direction that leads toward or fits a mature member of a biological species. If something is an armadillo, then it is already organizing changes in a good way, the way that fits the armadillo-type destination. This is why it makes sense to say, as mentioned in chapter three, "Be who you are." Nature sets a fitting direction for how we should live.

The Deduction Picture

The deduction picture is the view that we can start from some view about what human nature is like and deduce from it that humans ought to live by the moral law. Despite what I said in the previous section, I think this picture is a mistake. But before I get to my own objection, I want to admit that the most common objection to this picture is a bad one. Philosophers sometimes object to this picture in a crude way. They say, "The deduction picture violates a basic rule of logic. The rule is that you should not introduce into the conclusion of an argument any term not present in the premises. For example, if your premises say, 'All men are mortal' and 'Socrates is a man,' it is all right to conclude that Socrates is mortal. But it is not all right to conclude that Socrates is an armadillo. This is because the term *arma-*

dillo does not appear in the premises and so is not hooked up with the argument in the right kind of way. But the deduction picture presents an argument whose conclusion has the term *ought* in it ('humans ought to live by the moral law'), though this term has not appeared in any of the premises; the argument therefore violates this basic law of logic."

The trouble with this objection is that it begs the question against the deduction picture. It is bad practice in philosophy to start an argument with your opponent by simply denying him the use of his key ideas. If you do this, you have not won the argument against him but merely assumed from the beginning that he is wrong. It would be like arguing against belief in God, starting with the assumption that we cannot sensibly say or believe anything about God. The crude objection just mentioned fails to see that the deduction picture starts from the Aristotelian view of what it means to belong to a species like human (or armadillo). If something is a baby armadillo, in the Aristotelian view, then there is a direction it is supposed to follow to become a mature armadillo. The deduction picture sees morality as the way humans are supposed to live so as to reach mature humanity. But even if we dismiss the crude objection and accept the Aristotelian view of substance, a better objection to the deduction picture is still available.

The first sentence of Aristotle's *Nicomachean Ethics* is revealing here, since it gives a view in advance of the whole point of the book (as Aristotle's first sentences often do). "Every craft and every system, and likewise every action and decision, seems to aim at some good; hence the good has been well described as that at which everything aims." There is a problem here. Actions and decisions aim at an apparent good in the sense that we pursue what seems good to us. Perhaps our actions even aim at what could be actually good if we were in different circumstances. But not every action or decision aims at what is actually good for us and others in our actual circumstances. In fact, with a robust sense of human sinfulness, we will say that humans naturally aim toward the apparent but not the real good.

Humans (unlike armadillos) have choice; the inclinations we are born with, on this robust view of sin, prompt us not toward our chief good but, though we do not know it, toward our own destruction. There is a momentum toward evil as well as a momentum toward good. Chapter four described the basic conflict between putting the self first and putting first what is good in itself, and concluded that we are born with the first ranking rather than the second. This wrongful ranking has a momentum, in the sense that it gets progressively harder to break away from it. The self gets, as it were, more and more enclosed, and the habits of self-preference get more and more ingrained. Any signal from values outside us gets harder and harder to hear. We cannot therefore deduce a conclusion about how we ought to live from a premise about the inclinations we are born with or those we naturally develop. Chapter five distinguished between created nature and fallen nature. Human substance as created nature sets a fitting direction for us, though not a necessary one; however, human substance as we experience it is divided against itself.

If we look carefully at what Aristotle thinks humans are headed toward, we get some confirmation of this rather dark picture. I do not mean that Aristotle thought it was dark, but that we can see that what he thought was virtue (and hence a component of the human good toward which we are headed) is actually sin (and hence a path to human destruction). In the *Nicomachean Ethics* Aristotle says that those who have power over others and use it well (for example, the men who rule households and cities) have a more perfect kind of virtue than those who deliberate and act well only in what concerns themselves. In the *Politics* he says that only those who rule others need the full virtue of practical wisdom. The chief good of a human being, it thus turns out, requires having and exercising power over other human beings. This is an idea that can be found in many places in the Greek world, for example in Meno's summation in Plato's dialogue named after him, "(Virtue) must simply be the capacity to rule people, if you are looking for one quality to cover all the instances." That is fundamentally why Aristotle thinks slaves and women will never reach the chief human good. The same is true of manual workers, who are citizens but never have the resources for the kind of virtue Aristotle is talking about. Leisure, wealth, slaves and social position are all necessary for what Aristotle sees as the chief component of the chief good, namely contemplation. He is not saying that power over others is the whole or even the center of the chief good, but it is a necessary constituent.

Closely allied to power and riches is another requirement for excellence, as Aristotle sees it, namely prestige. Being well thought of is not, he says, the chief good. For it is possible to be well thought of by inferior people, and a person who aims merely at being well thought of will sink to their level. But Aristotle does think that prestige is necessary for the chief good. The magnanimous man thinks himself worthy of the greatest honor, and is worthy of it. The highborn, says Aristotle, and those who are powerful or wealthy, as long as they are not vicious, are esteemed worthy of honor; they are superior to their fellows, and superior excellence is always held in higher honor.

These goals of power and prestige are competitive. That is to say, if I am to have them, this requires that others do not (or at least have them less). But this "heading toward" power and prestige is inconsistent with the requirements of morality as I laid them out in chapter one. I do not mean to criticize Aristotle's claim that we are naturally headed toward those things, but I do mean to criticize his claim that because we are headed toward them, they are good for us to get. I think Aristotle is right about our natural inclinations. Though the particular forms they take are culturally specific (for example, Aristotle says the magnanimous man has slow movements, a deep voice and

calm speech), the underlying tendency is no doubt universal, or at
least universal for males. The qualification comes from Larry Arnhart,
whose views were discussed in chapter two. But it does not follow
that it is good for us and others that we get these things we aim at, or
that the prevailing cultural admiration for such things is right.

It is tempting to compare human beings to human artifacts, for
example, a car. You might think you could tell by looking at a car's
wipers what they are *for*. A good set of wipers is a set that performs
this function well. If a set of wipers is leaving smears on the windshield, we know they are not working properly. Here we get an
"ought" from an "is." Can we tell what humans are for just by looking at what they aim at and get an "ought" from an "is" in the same
way? But to get a proper analogy, we should suppose that the wipers
are not merely leaving smears but regularly reach in and smash the
windshield. Or that the engine produces large mechanical arms that
reach into the car and crush the passengers to death. If the car
behaved this way, could we tell by looking at how it behaved that it
was headed toward good? Human artifacts are not like this, because
we have designed them not to be, and we do not (because we cannot) give them freedom to disobey our instructions. But our designer
has allowed the artifacts (us) their freedom, and we have used this
freedom to betray the intentions of our designer. Our "is" is not yet
heading toward our "ought"; there is a gap to be bridged. Our nature
is now "fitted" for evil as well as good. We have to make a decision
between these two destinations, and we cannot (alas!) deduce from a
description of our existing direction that the direction is good.

God's Nonarbitrary Discretion

Why does it matter that we cannot deduce the moral law from human
nature? It matters partly because we are looking for a source of the
authority of morality; if the deduction picture were right, we would
have one. But also it matters because it affects how we see our relation

to God. If the deduction worked, it would follow that once God had created humans with the nature they have, even God would be logically forced to command that they follow the moral law. That is what deduction is like; it applies everywhere, even to God. Chapter one suggested that morality has two components: a set of norms (together with the values they respond to) and the organizing directive. There is a background to these in the norms given in the Ten Commandments on Mount Sinai and in the Sermon on the Mount and in the great command to love the neighbor as the self. In this book I am assuming that morality seen this way prescribes how all human beings should live. It is not intended only for some moral elite or only for Christians. The deduction picture claims that this morality as a whole is deducible from human nature. If it is, then even God cannot rightly command beings like us to do anything contrary to it. The only way to avoid this conclusion is to say that God can violate the laws of logic. Some philosophers have said this; however, it is an extreme position and leads to all sorts of counter-intuitive consequences, such as that God can be both God and not God.

It is better to think that God does not have to give us a particular set of commands, and that the divine sovereignty is not limited in this way. Instead we can think of God as choosing the moral law as a route toward our final destination, which is to be united with God. We can be grateful to God not only for creating us but also for giving us this excellent route (which God did not have to do). To take just one example, the eighth of the Ten Commandments forbids stealing, which presupposes the institution of private property. You can only steal what belongs to someone else. But it is presumptuous to say that God had to ordain private property. There have been human societies without it, and the members of those societies did not have to stop being human in order to live in them. The commandments are better seen not as a necessity binding God but as a route God chose for us.

Rosa constructs a treasure hunt for her daughter Lucy. The whole house and garden are transformed into a setting for the game, with each clue leading to the next in a preplanned sequence. If Lucy gets stuck, she can always ask her mother for help. But Rosa tries to plan it so that her daughter can work out what the clues mean on her own. The clues should make sense to anyone who knows the layout of the house and garden. The final clue leads to where the treasure is hidden. Because Rosa and Lucy love each other, the point of the game is not really to find the treasure (though that is how the game is set up). The game has a higher end, which is that the two of them enjoy each other. Rosa enjoys each stage of Lucy's discovery, and Lucy enjoys not just following the clues but her mother's enjoyment of the whole process as well. After the game it is this mutual delight that has been the greatest good. It is true that if Lucy does not find the treasure, both of them will be frustrated; but that is just the mechanics of the game, not what gives the game value. Once Lucy's cousin Chad came for a visit and took part in a treasure hunt. But he did not share in the love between mother and daughter. For him the treasure was the main point, and a disappointingly small treasure ruined the whole thing.

God's arrangements for our good might be like Rosa's arrangements for Lucy. There is no necessary way Rosa has to set up the game, though the final end consisting in some form of union is necessary. Once the clues are set up, then the route to the treasure is set, and it is our task to discover it. The treasure, the internal end of the hunt, is like one kind of happiness. There is a kind of life that is reached by truth telling and parent honoring and loving our enemies, and we discover that when we live this way we make progress and the world makes moral sense to us. If we will to live this way, we are repeating in our wills God's will for our willing. We are endorsing in our inside center what we take to be the objective requirements made on us from the external center that holds our lives and the whole universe together. But we should not deceive ourselves that we have discovered something necessitating God's will for our willing, that God had to will this way given the creation of beings with human nature. Finally, it is possible, like the visiting cousin, to be inordinately attached to the treasure that is the internal end of the game. As Duns Scotus says of the fall of Lucifer, it is possible to want the good to belong exclusively or preferentially to oneself.

There is another reason for preferring this picture, where the moral law is God's choice. Sometimes God is recorded in Scripture as commanding a violation of one of the Ten Commandments. For example, God commanded Abraham to kill his son Isaac. This is not an easy story to understand. An account in the New Testament (Heb 11:19) suggests that Abraham believed Isaac would come back to life and that both he and Isaac would be returning down the mountain, as he told his servants (Gen 22:5). But if we accept the deduction picture, then God could not have commanded Abraham to do any such thing, since it would have been a violation of the sixth commandment and thus necessarily wrong. Other such cases are the commendation of the Hebrew midwives (violating the ninth commandment), the command to the Israelites to take gold from the Egyptians under the threat of the plagues (violating the eighth) and the command to Hosea to marry Gomer the prostitute (violating the seventh). Moreover, God is reported in the Hebrew Scriptures to have commanded things (for example, wiping out the Canaanites) that are surely violations of the commands in the New Testament about how to treat our enemies. If human nature is fixed, and the moral law follows logically from it, how could God have commanded such things?

To say that the moral law is God's choice is not to say that it is optional for us. Once God has prescribed it as the route, it is indeed binding on us, unless God tells us otherwise. The point is just that it is possible for God to do this. This is what happened with the Hebrew ceremonial and dietary law, according to Christian tradition;

we are no longer required to keep the old laws about sacrifice and kosher food. The same thing could happen with the moral law. Regarding the eighth commandment, it is possible that in heaven there will be no private property. If so, this commandment will no longer apply; it will no longer be the route God prescribes. But we do not have to stop being human in order for this to happen. After Pentecost the early church abandoned private property and "had all things in common" (Acts 2:44). Some Native American tribes did not have the institution of private property. It may be that there was no private property before the Fall, but that does not mean that Adam and Eve were not human in the Garden of Eden. God can give humans different commands or prescribe a different route for different stages of human life. But in the deduction picture, where the moral law is deduced from human nature, God could not do this.

The Fitness of Morality
Nonetheless, although the moral law is not deducible from human nature, it fits human nature exceedingly well. We flourish when we keep it, and we deteriorate when we do not. Take the ninth commandment, which forbids bearing false witness. Because we are social and embodied animals, we need to communicate with each other by means of things like statements or pictures. And in order for this communication to work, we have to assume that we are saying to each other what we believe to be true. Imagine a mad professor who randomly said half the time things he believed true and half the time things he believed false. You would not learn anything from him, because you would never know what to put in your notes; every sentence could equally be something you should accept and something you should reject.

Lies are parasitic on the basic framework of truth telling in two senses. First, they cannot exist without this framework, just as a parasitic worm cannot live without its host. But second, they destroy the framework, again like the tapeworm killing its victim. As lies increase, communication becomes more difficult. Eventually, if people can no longer trust each other to say what they believe true rather than what they believe false, communication will stop. The ninth commandment therefore fits our nature as social beings extremely well, and lying damages it.

This point can be generalized to the other commandments God gives us, for example, in the second table of the Ten Commandments and in the Sermon on the Mount. One way to see this is to think about the truth of what Aristotle says about monsters. A monster is an aberration from a species form, for example, a two-headed pig. When we recognize something as a monster, Aristotle says, we show that we have a notion of how the species is supposed to be. The same is true with our recognition of moral failure. In recognizing something as a departure from how we are supposed to be, we show that we have a notion of something like an original design plan. A person who uses a beautifully prepared meal merely to fill his stomach is like a person who uses a well-honed chisel to remove screws. In both cases something fine is wasted and abused. In the same way, we have the ability to communicate so that we can share with each other our thoughts and intentions, and people who are good at it share their inner lives to an astonishing degree, making possible a rich and nuanced community of purpose. If we use this ability merely to deceive, we are wasting it. The same is true if we use sex merely for physical pleasure or use our parents merely as a source of funds or free lodging. The same is true if we use a proper hatred of evil as an excuse for hating an evildoer who has wronged us. In general we can see that failing to live by the commandments of God removes our chances at the kind of life that fits the best we can be and so fulfills us.

In the analogy of the treasure hunt, the treasure was like the life of truth telling and parent honoring and loving our enemies. It is significant that this is a single treasure. The various parts of the moral law belong together in a single integrated whole. If I am right about God's choice in this, we have here another reason for gratitude. God could have prescribed a route that was not integrated in this way. I will illustrate this with yet another analogy. The moral life is like a symphony written for an orchestra, and our capacities are like the instruments. The piece is not deducible from the nature of the instruments that play it. You cannot tell what the piece will be just by knowing what violins are like, and oboes, and trombones. But this particular piece shows off these instruments exceedingly well, and the contribution each instrument makes will be perfect for that instrument and its effect will depend on the perfectly tailored contributions of all the others. The piece is more vulnerable to breakdown than one that is not so well-adjusted to the different excellences of the different instruments. Imagine that one of the trombone players gets lost and wades in during the solo violin's haunting theme in the slow movement. Bach's *Art of the Fugue*, by contrast, is not scored for any particular instruments, and can be played successfully with hundreds of different combinations. It is a great piece of music, but it does not have this particular kind of integrity, in which the tonal quality of each part is precisely calibrated to work for the success of the whole. A morally good human life is more like the symphony.

Suppose a person is not good at telling the truth. Think of how this will affect his attempts to honor his parents and to be faithful to his spouse. Truthfulness is necessary for trustworthiness. Or think of how we are constantly besieged with the temptation to covet what does not belong to us. Resisting this temptation requires that we examine ourselves regularly and that we refuse to deceive ourselves about the real desires inside. But this in turn requires the habit of truthfulness to ourselves. Or think of how important and how hard truth is in the process of forgiving one's enemies. To forgive requires acknowledging in all its painfulness the harm that has been done;

otherwise forgiving an offense turns into condoning it. So the interdependence of the parts of the moral law gives us both greater risk of breakdown and the potential for greater reward, because of the kind of integrity it makes possible. A human moral life, if it is lived well, has an organic unity, the kind of unity that the armadillo's life has on Aristotle's picture, but much richer because it is so much more complex. All the parts are organized so as to make possible the whole, and no part could be deleted without making that particular kind of whole impossible.

The analogy of the symphony has suggested that the moral life is the same for every individual. But chapter one claimed that God's call is not only to human excellence but to an excellence which is unique to each person. Beethoven's *Fifth Symphony* can be played by different orchestras and sound quite different. One orchestra (like Philadelphia) will have a glorious string sound, and another (like Chicago) will be famous for its brass. Different conductors (like Bernstein and Furtwaengler) will take the same piece at different tempos and will emphasize different themes. The fitness between call and capacity applies at the individual level as well as the level of the species. God will call us to a unique excellence that fits our individual capacities exceedingly well.

There is also specialization by culture. It is good for all of us that the human family contains this kind of variety. There is a kind of parent honoring, for example, that is done in southern Zambia and in other societies with less personal mobility than the United States. Children stay with their parents as long as their parents are alive. No doubt moral benefits come from the freedom to change where we live more easily, but there are also moral costs. We start to think of people and relationships as disposable accessories like our clothes and furniture. And these costs are obscured by the very changes that produce the benefits. It is good for all of us to see the larger human picture with its differences and not assume that our own familiar way of leading the moral life is the only good one. We can be challenged to try to recover some of what we have lost, perhaps by simplifying the way we live and not throwing away lightly our bonds with other people. But even so, we should acknowledge that there are different good ways to follow the moral law, illustrated by those who live human life well in different cultures.

The commands God has given us fit our nature, but cannot be deduced from it. Even though it is hard for us to imagine a good human life that is not characterized by obedience to these particular laws, that is a defect in our imagination, not a requirement by which God is constrained. We have been trying to play this particular symphony all our lives, and we assume it is the only music that orchestras can play. But it is in fact possible to imagine humans without private property, where there are enough resources for all of us to flourish without it. We can imagine human life without marriage, as we are told human life will be in heaven. And we can imagine that our thinking might be immediately transparent to each other, so that there would be no need to construct external forms to communicate. The command to tell the truth would lose its application, since we would know straight away what others were thinking. We can certainly think of human life without enemies we have to love. The point is that we can form pictures of loving our neighbor in very different circumstances from those we now occupy, so we cannot be sure that the requirements of the particular commands God has given us are strictly inevitable for any fully excellent form of human life. We should be modest in our claims about what God has to tell us to do even given our present circumstances. Maybe there are constraints on what God could tell us to do in these circumstances, but we should be hesitant about saying we know what those constraints are.

We do not need to be so modest about the first of the two great commandments Jesus gives us, namely the command to love God with all our heart and soul and mind. In the analogy of the treasure hunt this was the higher end of the game, the mutual delight between Rosa and her daughter. It is possible for the internal end (the treasure) and the higher end to separate. This was the case with Chad, the visiting cousin, who could perhaps find the treasure (if he could ask Rosa for the necessary advice when he got stuck), but was not able to enter into the love between Rosa and her daughter. However, even though the internal end and the higher end can separate, this does not make their relation accidental or arbitrary. God has chosen the route for us as a route toward our final end, which is (as Scotus says) that we become co-lovers with God, entering into the love between the persons of the Trinity.

Returning to Raphael's fresco of the "School of Athens," we can say that he was right to insist on keeping Plato and Aristotle together at the focal point of the painting. We need Aristotle's emphasis that the forms (or natures) are in the world, but we also need Plato's emphasis on transcendence, not of the Forms, but of God. This is because the nature we are born with, which is Aristotle's kind of form, does not yet tell us which capacities and inclinations to fulfill to lead a good human life. Substance does set a fitting direction for how we should live, but it is substance as *created*, not the substance we encounter in our own nature as we live in human society. Without God's revelation we do not have access to a map (like the score of the symphony) of the ways our created nature has survived and the ways it has not.

Imagine that we did not have the life of Christ as an example. Would we know simply from analyzing human nature that we should love our enemies, and forgive seventy times seven times, and take on the role of becoming each other's servants? I think, on the contrary, we would reach roughly Aristotle's conclusions from studying our natural inclinations to power and prestige. Aristotle lived almost two and a half millennia ago, and the society he knew was in many ways different from ours. But his account of the kind of life we naturally look for still fits "common sense" in many ways better than the life Christ patterned for us, which is a radical reversal of some of the values we still find attractive.

Fulfillment is a kind of self-realization. But in our nature as we encounter it, we are divided between what we called in chapter five, following Kant, "the predisposition to good" and "the propensity to evil." So the activities that fulfill us or lead to self-realization are also divided. A life of wealth and high status is indeed fulfilling in many ways. But if we want to lead a morally good life according to the moral screening proposed in chapter one, we should not hanker for that kind of fulfillment. Martin Luther King Jr. said we should seek to be people who are, by the world's standard, "maladjusted." We should seek to serve and not to be served. We should seek to return injury with blessing. To someone like Aristotle, looking rationally at our natural inclinations, none of this makes sense. The widow who gives her last two small coins in the temple is, for Aristotle, not generous but stupid; she obviously cannot afford it. The Greek word for humility in the New Testament is used by Aristotle for the wretchedness that cannot even aspire to virtue.

When we reflect on all this, we can see that adjustment or fulfillment can be good or bad, depending on what we are adjusting to or what part of us we are fulfilling. We need something other than the human nature we are born with to tell us what fulfillment to seek and what not to seek. We need something that transcends our nature to play this role, and in the Christian tradition this is God's selection of the route toward our final end and God's revealing this in the life of Christ. In this picture, reaching that end will indeed fulfill us. When we get there, we will feel most completely ourselves, both in our common nature as humans and in our individual essence. But if I ask myself *now,* "What will make me feel most completely myself?" without appealing to revelation, I am going to get a divided answer.

In this picture it is not mere fulfillment that gives the moral route its authority, but God's selection and revelation of what kind of fulfillment is best for us.

8

Reason

Chapter five listed five different proposals for the source of the authority of morality. The present chapter looks at the third of these, reason. The main theme of the chapter is that our reason is limited in its access to information and in its ability to be impartial. This means that we cannot rely on it to tell us how to live. The conclusions of the previous two chapters can be expressed in terms of reason. We do not simply "see" with our reason the values that make for a good life and so "see" why we should try to be good. That was the claim of chapter six. Chapter seven argued that our reason does not simply discern our nature and deduce from it that morality is binding on us. The present chapter takes on the claims of reason more directly. The conclusion is the same as in the previous two chapters: we need something *above* our reason in order to recognize *in* our reason its proper value.

Chapter five also tied reason to significance by saying that we will sense that our lives have significance if they cohere with the central values we share with those around us. Our reason gives us the aspiration to this kind of significance. The present chapter denies that our reason by itself gives us sufficient grounds to hope for it, though faith can provide such grounds.

This chapter presents reason as pointing to an idealized position from which to think out what to do and how to live. This position is described in chapter one as "a position that can assess and that cares most about the well-being of the whole." But our reason will not be the source of the authority of morality, because while it points to this idealized position, it does not occupy it. Our reason is defective, and we therefore need to think of a reflection-position better than our own. The first section of this chapter makes the point that this position is not limited like us in its access to information. The second section adds that it is not limited by our tendency to prefer the self over others. The third section uses a version of an argument by Immanuel Kant that our reason not only points to an imagined position but requires us to have faith in an actual harmony of purposes that can give significance to a life. The final section argues that we need also the faith that our purposes are consistent with the unique flourishing of each person, but our reason is not sufficient by itself to ground this faith. As in chapters six and seven, the conclusion is that the proposed source for the authority of morality (in this case, reason) is not sufficient in the absence of belief in God.

Limits to Information

Rosa wants to buy a used car. Her current vehicle has reached the point where it is far more expensive to maintain than the car is worth. She visits some dealers, decides what model she wants and finally selects what seems to her the best deal, given the options she has seen. What would she count as an ideal position to be in when she makes this decision? It is easier to see what would count as a bad one. Suppose the car she buys turns out to be a lemon, though it looks good on the outside. She eventually has to have a completely new engine installed, and there is something seriously wrong with the transmission, which never does get fixed to her satisfaction. This would clearly be a nightmare, and to minimize the chances of this she takes the car to be checked by her usual mechanic before she buys it. Or suppose she buys the car and a week later discovers on another used-car lot an identical vehicle for a thousand dollars less. Again, a disaster. What these examples suggest is that she would make a good (a rational) decision if she had all the relevant information available to her before she made the deal.

This is a highly idealized picture. I have been helped to see this by Thomas Carson's book *Value and the Good Life*. When we see how much information is relevant, we can see that no human being could know all of it. Consider the car's insides. In order to know the merits of each vehicle, Rosa would have to know how good each of its components is. If the original paint job on the car was started on a Friday, stopped for the weekend, and started again on Monday morning, that is relevant information. If the steel alloy that the engine block is made of has a microscopic defect, that is relevant. If the previous owner once dropped a cigarette butt into the engine when changing the oil, that is relevant. This is all information about the vehicle's past, and the ideal position would be one that had access to all this information about all the cars that Rosa might buy. But the ideal position would also know about these vehicles' futures.

There are hard questions here about God's relation to time, and I have said that I do not understand this relation. But if it is possible for someone to know that a vehicle is going to break down completely in six months, then the person who has that knowledge is certainly in a better position than Rosa's. If knowledge of the future is impossible even for an omniscient God (as some philosophers think), it is still relevant to know the probabilities of the vehicle malfunctioning, and this is something we humans do not yet know how to estimate with any exactness.

No doubt a person can make a good decision about a used car without being omniscient. But if the question is, "What is the *ideal* position to be in when making such a decision?" the answer seems inevitably to be, "The position God is in, if there is a God." One way to see this is to compare making a decision in two different positions. In the first position we consider what we would prefer if we had all the information that was in fact available to us. In the second position we consider what we would prefer if we had full information. Since it is possible that there is important information that is now unavailable to us, most of us would prefer the second position to the first. But full information is available only to God, if there is a God.

Here is a second and related point. Rosa needs to know how likely it is that the sales agent is deceiving her about the merits of the car. Here she needs to know about human nature rather than the likely defects of car parts. She needs to know about the depravity that can infect even a quite ordinary person who makes a living by persuading people to buy expensive things that they do not understand very well. There is the same difficulty here as in the previous case about all the information necessary to be fully informed. But now there are some additional difficulties. This kind of information requires seeing into people's hearts. No doubt some humans are better than others at assessing character. However, none of us is very good even at seeing our own fundamental motivations. Moreover we would be harmed by the kind of knowledge this would give us. The veil that hides our thoughts from each other is, I think, merciful. Life would be unbearable if we knew all the time what people were thinking about us.

A third difficulty is that human minds are affected by the order in which information is presented to them and by how it is framed. There are many psychological studies that show that this happens, for example, when citizens are voting in an election. Patients who are told that an operation has a seventy percent chance of success are much more likely to go ahead with it than if they are told it has a thirty percent chance of failure. But the ideal position from which to make a decision would surely not be affected in this way. Moreover, we are influenced by the language in which information is described to us. Here I steal an example from J. David Velleman. If we are considering open-heart surgery, it makes a difference to us whether the operation is described to us in medical jargon like *incision, suture, clot* and *hemorrhage,* or in lay terms like *slice, sew, gob* and *gush.* There is a difference, also, if the information is presented in a verbal narrative or in full Technicolor on a screen. We want full vividness, but also enough emotional distance to preserve equanimity, and there may be no way to present the information to us that gets this balance right. These sorts of cases show in different ways that the human mind is not set up to achieve the ideal that we nonetheless try to approximate in our decision making.

The most telling difficulty is a fourth one. For humans, acquiring information has a cost. This may be straightforwardly a matter of buying a textbook or taking the time and effort to consult an expert. But there is also what economists call the "opportunity cost." If we are acquiring information, there is something else that we are not doing, and so something of value that we are sacrificing. Rosa goes to a certain number of car lots looking for the perfect car, but at some point she has to get on with her life. It is true that she might find the perfect car if her search covers a slightly larger geographical area, but she cannot afford the time to find out. Again, this is a limitation built into the human condition. We have the ideal of a position that is not limited in this way, and this ideal makes intelligible our efforts to get as close as we can and pay the information costs we have to pay. But we know that our lives contain more than just a single decision, and so we cannot afford the costs that would be necessary to get even all the information relevant to that one decision. We therefore compromise, putting roughly as much effort into unearthing the information for this one decision as we think this one decision is worth in the context of our lives as a whole.

Limits to Impartiality

So far we have been dealing with limits on our information. There is an equally significant limit on our commitment to impartiality. All of the four limitations thus far considered apply to people's decisions about what is best for themselves. But as described in chapter one, morality does not allow people to give more weight in the decision to themselves than to anyone else they might affect by what they do. Every person counts as one, and no person as more than one. A moral person, according to chapter one, is concerned for the well-being of human beings seen as having equal value. The problem is that we hardly ever accord this kind of equal value to people.

Partly this is again a matter of limited information. To treat another person as having equal value with ourselves requires sharing her or his morally permitted ends (or purposes), making those ends our own. But we often do not know what those ends are, so we cannot share them. In fact, the situation is worse than this. Not only do we not know what those ends are, but we impute ends to other people, assuming them to be either like ourselves or like some stereotype we have in our minds. Here is an example of the first kind. If I tend toward an exaggerated desire for personal privacy, I will tend to assume that a person I see sitting at a table in the lunchroom by himself does not want to be disturbed; I will choose another table that is empty. On the other hand if I am unusually gregarious, I will tend to interpret the signs he gives as meaning that he wants company, and sit down at the table beside him. The person himself may have behaved in an identically neutral way both times, neither encouraging more contact nor discouraging it; however, I project my own desires onto him as though he were a mirror, reflecting me to myself. A stereotype works in a different way, projecting a stock picture onto a person. I assume when I learn that the woman I am sitting next to is an Episcopalian that she will not want to share my lowly Velveeta and pickle sandwich.

In order to know the purposes of another person so that I can make them my own, I have to be able to see into her heart. And the only person who is in a position to do that is God, if God exists. So partly the moral problem is one of not knowing other people well enough. But suppose I do have at least a rough idea of another person's purposes. Then another difficulty arises: I have to give them the same importance as my own.

Rosa knows fairly clearly that the person next to her on the bus is hungry. He eyed her Velveeta sandwich with longing when she took it out of her travel bag. The question is whether she is going to offer him half of it. She is very hungry herself, and this is hard; however, she can manage it because she has the virtue profile described in chapter one. She feels good when she has done it (though she did not do it in order to feel good about it). But when she reaches the downtown bus station, she is faced with need on a much larger scale. She is transferring to another bus, and the person sitting next to her in the terminal has probably been there all night, perhaps for several nights. He is hungry too, and the thought occurs to her that she could offer him breakfast at the coffee shop. But he is not the only person around her who needs her help. A woman in the row of chairs opposite is sighing continually and deeply. Rosa wonders whether she should go over and listen to her story. She doesn't want to interfere, but she wonders about the letter the woman keeps turning over and over in her hands. Doesn't she need a friendly ear?

Here is the whole problem in miniature. How much importance is Rosa allowed to give to her desire for a bit of peace and quiet in the middle of a long and tiring trip? May she really treat herself and her own needs as no more important than anyone else's? I do not pretend to know where the balance lies in this case. But the point I am making is that she doesn't know either, despite her many virtues. The position she is imagining is one in which all the people involved, including herself, are loved the same. But that is not a position she in fact occupies. It is the position God occupies, if God exists. What she would like to know is God's will for her willing. This is a problem for Rosa even in buying her used car. How many extra features is it good for her to seek in a vehicle? Is the basic stripped-down version enough, or may she insist on air-conditioning, or a sun roof? The answer depends partly on how important her own comfort is, since she will be the one driving the car.

Chapter one described the moral gap as having two elements: the moral demand and our (defective) natural capacities. It added that many people join a third element to the first two, a possible holy being who is seen as the source of the demand. We can now see why reason might require this third element in the picture.

A Harmony of Purposes

So far the ideal of reason has been presented as merely an ideal, a possible standpoint that we imagine as a kind of measure for us to approximate. But reason gives us more than merely an ideal. Chapter four already laid out some of the background for this claim. If we are going to persevere in the moral life, reason requires that we believe in the consistency of the ends we pursue. This consistency puts constraints not merely on what we imagine but also on what we believe to be real.

Rosa's life contains some inconsistent purposes. They are inconsistent not intrinsically but because of the situations she finds herself in. At her friend's cello recital he plays Bach, and he puts in some of those little romantic slides that she so much dislikes. Should she say something about this when she sees him after the concert? Yes and no. She wants to encourage him and to say nice things about his performance. On the other hand, he has been guilty of a serious error of taste, and he should not be allowed to get away with it. She values truthfulness and feels uneasy whenever she is put in a situation that calls for less than the whole truth. These purposes are inconsistent because now she is in a situation in which she cannot satisfy all of them, and she has to choose.

This is true also when she shares the ends of other people. She values very much a particular group of friends that she has, but she is worried that it becomes cliquish. She also has a rather awkward friend, Beth, who would like to be part of the group but who does not seem to be able to get along with the others. Rosa wants to share the morally permitted ends of all her friends, and this means making those ends her own ends. When she finds out from Beth and her other friends what they want, however, this sharing puts her in a quandary. How can she make it her end both that Beth join the group and that Beth not join the group?

What reason requires is not that people's initial ends or purposes be consistent but that they believe in the consistency of the ends they decide to pursue. When we decide on some good we intend to pursue, we have to believe that we can achieve that good (not necessarily by our own resources alone). We do not usually pursue a good in isolation, but against the background of other goods we want together with it. It is often these other goods that make sense of our pursuit of the first one. These other goods give the first one its overall meaning.

Rosa wants to encourage her cellist friend. This desire makes sense against the background of a set of values that she has, first described in chapter one and expanded in subsequent chapters. She decides in this case that she will say something about the little slides because she cannot be true to the friendship and dishonest about the music, which they both love and which is one of the foundations of their pleasure in each other's company.

Here there is a pattern or network of goods, and the friendship and the love of music and the truthfulness are all bound up in it. The friendship does not make sense outside this pattern. It is not and could not be an isolated good pursued by itself. Friendship is always a shared valuation of something beyond the friendship itself. Meaning or significance in a life is given by this pattern of goods. Values do not all have the same significance-conferring power. Values with more of this power, like the value of good music, confer significance on those with less. Often the values that have more power will be shared in the community that a person belongs to and in the relationships that are important to him or her. When Rosa decides on an action, she is endorsing the pattern of goods that gives this action its significance. But then she has to believe that this pattern of goods is coherent in the sense that it is achievable together (though not necessarily by her resources alone).

Not all people have the same degree of integration in their desires, but integration is a sign of maturity. In *The Moral Gap* I distinguished between Tiggers (who have a high intensity of desires, taken singly, but not much integration between them) and Eeyores (who have a high degree of integration but a lower degree of intensity, desire by desire). I suggested that there is a typical development from adolescence to middle age in which Tigger-like desires wear each other down (like sharp stones in a mechanical polisher) until they lose their edges. The fifty-year-old knows herself better, and knows that there are alternative ways to reach what she values. She is not as distraught as the adolescent when one of these ways is blocked.

Integration is not the same as an overall hierarchy of desires. Like some contemporary philosophers, the nineteenth-century philosopher Friedrich Nietzsche denied the need for a transcendent standpoint from which to judge our values, and was happy drinking his cup of cocoa each morning—a small good not given its meaning by any larger story about the moral purpose of his life or the universe as a whole. But even Nietzsche (like the adolescent) has to believe that his eventual purposes, though disparate, are consistent with each other to a large extent. Consider the possibility of a demon who delighted in mucking up our practical lives, so that whenever we aimed at some good he would dump on us some evil that we hated to a somewhat higher degree than we loved the good. Imagine that whenever Nietzsche sat down to drink his hot chocolate, the demon would appear in the guise of a boring metaphysician and would not go away before being granted twenty minutes of conversation. Alas, that would be the end of the cocoa! Now suppose that the demon does not always do this with Nietzsche's purposes, but most of the time or half the time. It would be like the mad professor (mentioned in chapter seven) who randomly told his students half the time what he thought was true and half the time what he thought was false. The students would not be able to learn anything in his course. The same would be true if we were victims of the demon, only this time our fate would be that we would not be able to deliberate about what to do. There would be no point to it.

Although there are good things, like Nietzsche's hot chocolate, that are comparatively isolated from a larger pattern of values, these probably do not have the power to sustain a person's interest in life. This is the paradox of the aesthete's life as Søren Kierkegaard describes him in *Either/Or*. Kierkegaard imagines him as a look-out at the top of a ship's mast when waves are crashing on the deck below. The ship is a metaphor for his own life. The sight of the deck from above is interesting, but he is not engaged with it and does not want to be engaged with it. The pilot of the ship, on the other hand, has to make decisions about how to face the storm. The paradox is that the aesthete cannot sustain his interest without engagement. The very things that make a life interesting are the things that are larger than he is and that require commitment. These are things like marriage or a worthwhile job. The aesthete wants to be disengaged, or detached, enjoying his small aesthetic pleasures one at a time, without any larger narrative that makes sense of them. Kierkegaard's point is that such a life is in the end merely boring.

Coherence in our ends is made harder when we consider the ends we take on from other people. This is the problem with Beth and the clique. Again Rosa opts for truthfulness even though it is painful. Her friendship with the group is founded on a certain kind of openness and sensitivity, which the others are violating. Rosa thinks that if the others just let Beth in, perhaps she will find a way to become a valued member of the group, though maybe not right away. And even if it doesn't work, at least they should try. So she tells her friends that she is not going to stay with them if they insist on keeping Beth out. She is envisaging a certain state of the world that has the group continuing happily with Beth as a new member (though maybe the group will have to change a bit). If Rosa is going to act on this vision, she has to believe that this state of the world is possible.

But now consider the larger sphere in which she lives her life. She affects hundreds of people as she drives and shops and teaches her students. She has to believe that she can achieve her purposes consistently with them achieving theirs (as long as their purposes are not morally forbidden). The world might be the kind of place in which some can be happy only if most are not, or in which Rosa can only be happy if others are not. She has to believe the world is not like this. As in chapter four, "she has to" means that she has to if she wants a coherent view. Perhaps many people do not even consider the matter, but this belief is nonetheless implicit in how most of them go about their lives.

In thinking about how people's happiness can fit together, we have a massive coordination problem. Rosa has to believe in not just an imagined ideal but a real harmony of purposes; what can explain such a harmony? This question is a moral version of the question about the order of the cosmos as a whole. *Cosmos* is a Greek word that can be

translated "harmony." We can ask, What explains the cosmic order?
Some people will answer, Well, it just is, and we do not need an
explanation. However, the problem is that there is so much physical
evidence of forces and elements that make the existence and survival
of this cosmos hard to explain. We feel the need to bring in something
else, something that we do not understand, to explain how nonetheless the cosmos came into being and continues to exist. In the same
way in the moral sphere some people will say that the harmony of
purposes just is. But we see forces in the individual and in society
leading away from harmony. Christian doctrine calls them collectively
"sin." We need some explanation for what counters these forces and
harnesses the good in us toward harmony.

Chapter four proposed for this role the doctrine of providence in a
moralized form, defining providence as "a moral ordering behind or
within the universe, which allows it to make moral sense." This
ordering does not have to be done by God, though the Christian tradition gives this role to God, both in the scientific and the moral
realms. Abraham Kuyper writes, "The coherence of things is their
original relation with God." Chapter four asserted that this ordering
is consistent with our experience of tragedy. There is enough evil in
the world so that sometimes we have no good options but only a
choice of bad ones. Certainly people's purposes are often not con-
jointly achievable if, for example, one group wants to kill as many as
possible of another. Nonetheless, belief in providence is belief that
tragedy is not all there is; the good in the world is more fundamental
than the evil and will in the end prevail. I think that if we believed
that tragedy was the whole story, we would not be able to sustain the
moral life.

There are many different pictures of what providence might be
like. I will briefly and schematically give three ways of connecting it
with God, starting with the least ambitious in terms of how much we
have to believe. The first sees God acting entirely within human

beings (or other living things). The second sees God acting within the universe, but as a force acting on human beings (or other living things), not merely inside them. The third sees God not merely as acting within the universe, but also acting as an agent on the universe.

First, we might think of God within human beings collectively as a spirit that binds them together, a kind of "holy spirit." Each human has his or her own irreplaceable value, and to the extent that we recognize this value we activate this holy spirit in ourselves and stimulate it in each other. God is not transcendent in this picture. But God is nonetheless more than any individual or even than their sum. For God is the spirit that reaches out beyond how we actually live toward a life in which we all recognize each other's irreplaceable value. We could think of providence here as a kind of momentum toward solidarity, generated from our lives to the extent that we live morally well. We can include more than just humans, if we think of other things in the world living as it is good for them to live. If all life in the universe were to end, however, God would end too, according to this picture.

Or we might think of God as still within the universe—not merely within living things, however, but a force like love acting on them. Perhaps this force actually brings life into being in the first place. Chapter two discussed such a possibility in the final section. An analogy might be the currency flowing in and out of an enormous bank. Deposits can be made into the bank and withdrawals made from it, but the currency is not money but love. Love has the power to alter the people loving as well as the people loved. Providence in this picture would be more active than providence in the previous picture. In terms of the analogy it secures the storage and transfer of the currency. In this bank, one person can deposit and another person can (to some extent) withdraw the funds. In this way the ends of the different users of the bank are coordinated with each other. God has a kind of transcendence in this picture. God is not confined to living substances, but acts on them from outside them. However, if the universe were to end, in this picture God would end with it.

Or finally, we might think of God as an agent acting on the universe from beyond it. One image is God as king or sovereign. It is hard in the modern world (especially for Americans) to imagine what it is like to have a king. But we can picture that Rosa has in her classroom-kingdom legislative, executive and judicial power. She is not a tyrant, but she supervises her students' education from a position over them. In this picture, providence is the teacher's "providing" of curriculum (her legislative authority), her daily implementing it and her caring for the students' individual needs (her executive authority) and her appropriate rewarding and punishing (her judicial authority). In this way she harnesses the students' purposes (initially disparate and often in conflict) to create a healthy learning environment for all of them. Rosa's existence does not depend on the existence of the students, however. She existed perfectly well before becoming their teacher.

Christianity has elements of all these pictures. God is in the universe, both within us and a force on us, and is also beyond the universe. What all three pictures have in common is that individual members of the "kingdom" to which we belong are helped by something larger than any of us to form a coherent whole. "Providence" is a name for this something. Our reason requires us not merely to imagine this as an ideal but to believe it is actually in place even though our reason does not have in itself the capacity to provide it for us.

Reason and the Particular

Finally we can return to another problem raised in chapter five about the limits of reason. That chapter suggested that morality is irreducibly particular, and we looked at the example of Rosa and Lucy's shoes. Some philosophers think that reason deals only with universals, namely, what is or can be common to different things and different times and places. Suppose I throw a rock at a window. Reason in science is concerned with laws that govern the impact of any projectile with a certain mass and velocity on any surface of a certain fragility. Maybe we can see or touch the particular rock or the particular window that got us started. But when we reason about the impact, we move to a more abstract level at which the particular objects are mentioned no longer and only the law is left, applying to any objects of the relevant kind. No doubt science does more than this. But if this is our model of what reason is like, then reason does not cover the whole of morality. It does cover the part of morality that deals with laws and rules. But in terms of this distinction, there is also a part of morality that is more like seeing or touching. Rosa has a moral relation to Lucy that is tied essentially to her. It cannot be captured in any statement of obligation that drops reference to Lucy and replaces it with reference to anyone who is her daughter, and is seven years old, and is in distress, and so on. The moral relation ties Rosa to Lucy's individual essence, even though Rosa knows this only partially and in fragments.

Shakespeare has a famous sonnet that begins:

> Let me not to the marriage of true minds
> Admit impediments. Love is not love
> Which alters when it alteration finds,
> Or bends with the remover to remove.

This sonnet presents a remarkably high ideal of true love. Some contemporary critics have either dismissed it as "inane," as "bombast" or as mere conventional piety; or they have proposed a reading according to which the speaker of the poem is desperately pretending to himself that he does not know what we all know, that love is not like that at all. But the Christian tradition of which Shakespeare is a part teaches that we are capable, with God's assistance, of a kind of unconditional love that is committed to not altering when the other person alters and not removing when the other person removes. That is why this poem is often read at marriage services, to accompany the vows "for richer, for poorer; in sickness and in health."

It is hard, however, to say what the *object* of such a love can be. Do I love my true love for herself alone? I get into difficulty either way. If I say it is her characteristics that constitute the reason for loving her, I seem to be denying her unique individuality. She can complain, "You only love me for my raven hair." On the other hand if I say, "You are loved not for your characteristics but simply because you are you," this divorces her "youness" from all her characteristics, including those that are most familiar and most dear to me and that seem most intimately tied to who she is. If there really is this kind of unconditional love, it has to have as its object something both essential and at least glimpsed, and the individual essence seems the perfect candidate. If my true love loses her raven hair to chemotherapy, and if she even loses her familiar character and personality, I can still love her with this kind of love. Given some changes, we may not be able to stay in the same house, and the ideal seems wrongly stated as "no alteration." I may need to relate to her differently; but I can still love her.

I am faced with this question when as a church elder I visit an elderly member of my congregation in a nursing home, and she does not respond to me, or apparently to anyone. Whom am I trying to love? Is she still there in the bed? I am less likely to think of her as gone if I recognize that I do not know except in fragments what makes her the individual she is and that only God knows this.

How can I love if I do not understand what I am loving? Here it is useful to think about how we love God even though we do not fully know or understand the essence of God. We know some things about this essence, that God is necessarily omniscient and omnipotent and loving. But what ties these characteristics together into a single divine nature in three persons, we do not understand. We can still love what we do not understand. And the same is true with other people; we can love them without knowing their individual essences. Philosophers who think this way tend to emphasize the will, which is the seat of love, over the intellect, which is the seat of understanding. One way to put the difference is to ask whether our final state will be one of loving God or one of seeing God. No doubt it will be both, but it makes a difference which of these we emphasize. I think the seeing is introductory to the loving. When we love a person, on this view, we seek her good. But that good can only be known perfectly by someone who knows her essence. God knows this completely, and we cannot; however, we can know enough to love her.

We want our lives to be significant. Can our own reason give us this significance, or ground our belief that we have it? The third section of this chapter suggested that significance comes from living within a pattern in which the goals that we pursue are by and large consistent with each other and with our values, which make sense of them. This is especially true if the values are shared in the communities we belong to and the relationships we care about. In this way Rosa's love of music makes sense of her maintaining her friendship with the sentimental cellist. Knowing that there is such a pattern requires a view of the whole, a view that is not limited in information and impartiality in the way our own view is limited. Our reason prompts the desire for this kind of significance, but it cannot ground the belief that our lives are in fact significant in this way. Immanuel Kant put it like this: Our reason has the peculiar fate of being given by its own nature the burden of answering questions that because of the very same nature it is unable to answer. We therefore have to have faith, faith that we can affirm that our lives are significant, even if we cannot now see how all the various purposes we and others pursue work together. Belief in God grounds such a faith by placing the origin of this consistency in God's will.

This final section of the chapter adds a new point. We have only fragmentary knowledge of the individual essences that make all of us what we are. The previous chapter suggested that our created nature as human beings directs us toward a fitting life; I think the same is true of our individual natures. God, in giving us our unique name, is giving us a direction that is unique to us. If we think of reason as necessarily concerned only with what is universal or potentially common to different things, then reason will not have access either to the individual essence or to the unique direction. Even if we allow that reason has a very partial and fragmentary access to what is unique to each individual, we still need faith. We need faith that what we pursue is consistent with the unique well-being of each of the people we affect by our actions, including ourselves. This faith is assisted by locating the call to morality in the will of a person who knows and loves what each of us in our essence is.

9

Community

Chapter eight claimed that human reason does not provide the source of the authority of morality. Our reason does, however, give us the aspiration toward a kind of significance in our lives that belief in God helps us reach. This present chapter makes the same kind of argument about another candidate source for the authority of morality: community. Someone might think community is a good candidate because the demands of morality often come to us through the communities we belong to. When we conform to community standards, we get a sense of belonging together with people we care about, and one of the fruits we seek from morality is that it should hold us together in this kind of mutually supportive life.

Community also seems like a plausible candidate because it ties together the needs we have already met for transcendence, fulfillment and significance. Community has a positive role in meeting all three of these needs, but this role can be exaggerated. The remaining sections of this chapter argue that community by itself cannot provide a foundation for morality, but we need to look for that in a source beyond our community. We will examine various kinds of difficulty we get into when we try to make community play that role by itself.

Transcendence was the topic of chapter six, together with the idea of a "magnetic center" outside ourselves that we respond to in our evaluations. The community too transcends the life of the individual member. We see this clearly in wartime, or in an emergency in a city, when people can subordinate remarkably their individual ends to the good of the whole. In some exaggerated versions of this view the individual is seen as no more than an organic part of the community, as a bodily organ is part of the whole organism. This organic view, when taken by itself, fails to recognize the integrity of each individual. Nonetheless it is true that the community stops us getting stuck inside ourselves. When we see ourselves meeting the needs of the people around us, and when we see them meeting our needs, we can see that we belong together to something bigger than any one of us. Loyalty is the response to this value outside us when we feel it overriding our individual self-interest.

Chapter seven focused on fulfillment, together with the idea of deriving morality from human nature. The person who is part of a community fulfills her or his nature as a social animal. There is again an exaggerated way to put this. Aristotle talks as though we always fulfill our nature when we give priority to our community over ourselves. But sometimes this kind of self-quashing defeats us. We need to be able to see our own value over against the community we belong to so that we can resist its demands when they become overbearing. Nonetheless it is true that the community enables us to fully use that part of our nature. Even the solitary hermit in the desert is connected through prayer to those outside his cave. The moral virtues are all defined interpersonally, and most of them require a community for their exercise. A sizeable part of what makes life worth living comes to us through close connections with other people.

Finally, significance was the topic of chapter eight; there we examined the meaning that is given to our individual purposes by their integration into a larger whole. The community gives us larger narratives into which we can place our lives, for example, the story in Christianity of sin and redemption or the story in Marxism of the triumph of the working class. These narratives give us a context within which to make sense of our own successes and failures as they happen to us. In exaggerated versions of this point, the stories that come from a larger social context are seen as sufficient to give meaning to our lives, as though all we have to do is to belong to a community with a good story. But meaning-in-a-life (like most kinds of meaning) comes by applying the general to the particular, and we have to shape our individual stories by our choices and decisions. Nonetheless it is true that the community gives us the material to shape and apply in this way, and without it we could not get underway with the project of making sense of our lives.

Given all this great benefit from belonging to a community, we can see how people who do not believe in God might think community is the foundation of morality. However, making community the source of the authority of morality leads to relativism and exclusivity. A section of this chapter addresses each of these points. If seen against the background of some theological premises, however, the true moral value of community can be appreciated. The key idea, which will end this chapter, is that community can play its proper moral role if we see it as a providential gift. This belief enables us to overcome the tendencies (I think most of us feel both of them) to be too attached to our community and to be too detached from it.

Relativism

The first difficulty with overvaluing community is one already mentioned in chapter five. If we say that the community is the source for the authority of morality, we will have to say which community we are talking about. At the beginning of this book I commented on the different worlds of Homer, Virgil, the author of *Beowulf,* and Milton, who lived at intervals of about eight centuries from each other. The same point can be made in terms of geographical spread and the different kinds of life people live in Grand Rapids, Michigan, and in Njola, a village in southern Zambia. In Njola, each family eats the food they grow. In Grand Rapids, when I eat a kiwi fruit, it has been fed by water diverted two hundred miles in California, fertilized by a large mechanical fertilizer, harvested by a migrant laborer, shipped to a warehouse where it is wrapped in paper or plastic and stickered and boxed, and then trucked two thousand miles, shelved in a supermarket, slipped into paper or plastic by the bagger and then driven to my house.

One version of relativism is expressed in the saying "When in Rome, do as the Romans do." The first thing to point out is that this kind of relativism is a normative claim and not merely a descriptive one. Chapter one made this distinction in terms of different ways to understand the question "What is morality?" Normative ways to understand the question are "What norms *should* we live by?" or "What norms are morally permitted?" The descriptive way is "What norms *do* we live by?" We can ask that descriptive question about other cultures as well: "What norms do they live by?" There is a descriptive kind of relativism, which claims merely that different cultures *do* live by different norms. I think this merely descriptive claim is true. This was the point about Homer and Milton, Grand Rapids and Njola. But if I say, "When in Rome, do as the Romans do," I am telling someone what to do. I am not de-scribing, I am pre-scribing. So, for example, Homer's epic records that the Greeks, after defeating the Trojans, burnt the city to the ground, killed all the men of fighting age, and sold all the women and children into slavery. If relativism is understood normatively, it means that the Greeks were morally permitted to do this, for the view is that the values of a society justify its practices, or make them right.

The same would be true about our own society. If relativism is understood normatively, it means that our society's valuation of convenience and accessibility justifies the use of all those resources to get me my kiwi fruit. But there is no reason to believe the dominance of an idea in a society confers moral rightness on it. The dominant norms in a society will indeed have power, but power is not the same as moral authority. In the same way a political regime can have power and maintain it by ruthless oppression; however, this does not mean that the regime has a moral right to the obedience of the people it has oppressed.

There are some bogus reasons why normative relativism may seem attractive. Here are three: The first is that it may seem to lead to tolerance. I have found this view among some of my students. They hate the kind of imperialism that leads people to impose their views on others, the way Europeans imposed their views on the nations they conquered and "civilized" in the eighteenth and nineteenth centuries. My students respond by saying that we must leave each people to its own ways. They think that this kind of tolerance comes from normative relativism. But normative relativism doesn't lead to tolerance. It is committed to treating tolerance just like any other norm; whether the norm is right or not depends on what society you belong to. The ancient Greeks were not at all tolerant in the modern sense. They coined the term *barbarian*, which means literally people who sound like "bar ... bar ... bar" when they talk; in other words, people who don't speak Greek. The Greeks made such people, when they conquered them, into slaves. Normative relativism is committed to saying that there is nothing wrong with the Greeks doing so.

The second bogus reason for the attraction of normative relativism is a confusion between the question whether some practice is wrong and the question whether we should forcibly intervene to stop it.

Sometimes we probably should intervene; for example, we should intervene to stop genocide. However, the imperialists intervened in the name of "civilized" values when they were not morally justified in doing so and were pursuing their own commercial interests. But the fact that this intervention was wrong does not show that all the customary practices in the conquered nations (such as female infanticide or burning widows alive) were morally permitted.

Third, some people think that the large variety of social norms itself shows that all those norms are morally permissible. But why should it show this? Compare the variety of scientific views that have been held at different times in history. Aristotle believed, for example, that the sun went round the earth, and he was typical of his time. But it does not follow from the fact that there have been many different scientific beliefs over the history of science that all these beliefs are true. No more does it follow from the variety of social norms over history that all those norms are morally permissible. Perhaps someone can show how science is different from ethics, so that in science truth is objective and in ethics it isn't. For example, someone might argue that science has a kind of convergence toward consensus in a way that ethics does not. But there has in fact been a remarkable spread of Western ethical ideas, very similar to the spread of Western science. In neither case does the convergence alone prove truth, because it could be due as much to power as to intrinsic authority. The point is that both variety and convergence in both science and ethics are consistent with some beliefs being objectively true and others being false. Variety in social norms does not prove that *normative* relativism is true.

When we make a moral judgment, we are in the standard case endorsing or refusing to endorse an attraction or repulsion toward something. Chapter six offered Plato's example of the performer of Homer's poems who laughs inside even as he transmits the grief from the poet to the audience. Often the attraction will come to us clothed in language and concepts we inherit from our culture. Moral judgment can have the critical function of distancing us from the culture we grew up in. My nanny told me that gentlemen polish the backs of their shoes, and my scout told me that gentlemen keep their rooms in good order. Because gentlemen brush their hair, I was beaten at school by a prefect for coming down to breakfast with my hair unbrushed.

My shoe backs are now unpolished, my room untidy, and my hair for the most part unbrushed, and I make the judgment that all this should not have the kind of symbolic value it did in the country where I grew up. I am not being merely rebellious (though I expect that is part of it); rather, I have used the screening procedure described in chapter one. I now think that the system that divides a society into gentlemen (and ladies) and the rest, and gives the greatest privileges to the gentlemen (and ladies), does not treat all human beings as having unique and equal value. This conclusion needs a complex argument, which I will not try to give here. The point is that because moral judgment has this critical function, the community in which a person is born is not the source of the authority of morality.

A natural reply to this is as follows: The very ideal of human equality you have just appealed to is itself a cultural construct, part of the very same cultural mix as the class system you have been objecting to. As you said in chapter one, not all cultures have this ideal. Homer's did not. So you are not really departing from your culture when you condemn it for class snobbery. The truth is that you are using one part of your culture against another.

Part of this I have to agree with. The moral screening procedure described in chapter one is not my invention. It comes to me through cultural sources such as my parents, my teachers, books I have read and churches I have attended. Even original ideas come to us through culture in this way and are to a large extent recombinations of elements that were already present. Maybe God can give some people an idea or a "word" by revelation, and then give them an accompanying understanding of that word that is not dependent on their prior understanding of the language and culture in which they live. I do not know whether that happens or not. But it is not what happened for me with the idea that all humans have equal dignity. It came to me through the cultural influences to which I have been exposed.

However, it does not follow from this that the idea is merely a cultural construct. Chapter six argued against the view that evaluation is always projection, that we create the values we live by and project them onto the world, in the way Despina projected her contempt onto the poor people she found contemptible. The view that we create all our ideas is a similar mistake. We reach some of them because they fit what we experience, though we may not be able to sort out completely how we have modified this input by our interpretation. Some scientific beliefs are true, for example, and some are false, even though both kinds can be expressed in the same language and can belong to the same cultural tradition. I think scientists assume that their true theories are not simply their invention, and that these theories correspond in some way to the things in the world that they are about.

How can we tell which norms are right and which are not? Chapter one suggested a moral screening procedure. But how can we tell which screening procedure is right? One thing we can do is to look for fitness in the two kinds of center described in chapter six: inside and outside. Internal fitness is internal to a person's will. A sign of this kind of fitness in that the screening procedure has sorted out successfully the desires and purposes that the person has continued to be able to identify as his or her own. Often this becomes clear at moments of tension. For example, Rosa had to insist that her group of friends not exclude Beth, she had to tell her cellist friend that he was abusing Bach, and she had to apologize to Lucy about the shoes. At these times, she felt stress between different things she wanted, and she had to work through it. If when she looks back she can see that the screening procedure allowed her to hang onto the things that have really mattered, that is a sign it has worked well. This kind of comfort does not constitute complete proof because it is always possible that she has merely deteriorated, like the springs of an old chair, and has become content with less moral aspiration than she should. But still, it is positive evidence.

External fitness is a relation to the magnetic center outside a person. The screening procedure aims to retain the signals that come to him from this center and to exclude the ones that do not. He might come to doubt the procedure if he realizes that it has been letting in values he now rejects. He will be reassured if he can find people using the same screening procedure in different cultures. For example, he judges his original class-conscious culture to be defective, and he can see a more egalitarian North American culture that (though it may be inferior in other ways) is less snobbish in applying the screening he originally learned through his own culture. This means the screening procedure is not necessarily corrupted by its association with a class structure. Again this is not a proof, for error can be shared between cultures just as much as truth. We have to retain a humble acceptance of the possibility that we have the wrong procedure. But still, this kind of sharing is positive evidence.

The kind of moral screening we have been discussing is embedded historically in the context of Christianity. Over the last couple of centuries there has been an attempt to detach it from this context. This means that we are presented in the current situation with a choice about whether to retain this context or to discard it. When a person is faced with competing worldviews, there is a question she can ask: Does each of them contain the resources to understand and provide an account of the failures and defects of the other? Sometimes this is not the case. For example (to simplify a complex transition mentioned in chapter four), we can observe historically how Homer's worldview gave way in the ancient Greek city states to a more democratic form of governance, and how this produced in turn the kind of love of country we see in the person of Aeneas in Virgil's epic. About a century after the Homeric poems were written down, we find the conservative poet Theognis lamenting how the class structure has been subverted. He was resisting the transition to the new order, and so gives us an inside picture of the forces arrayed against each other:

> Unchanged the walls, but, ah, how changed the folk!
> The base, who knew erstwhile nor law nor right,
> But dwelled like deer, with goatskin for a cloak,
> Are now ennobled; and, O sorry plight!
> The nobles are made base in all men's sight.

But the realities of the new social order had allowed a new understanding by the nonnoble folk of their own value, and the traditional picture could not account for this. The new picture could understand very well the kind of oppression they had been subjected to.

Not all cultural transitions are accomplished by reason. Sometimes they are brought about by force rather than persuasion. But the choice between worldviews can be given some nonrelativistic grounding if we see that one of them is better at understanding the other. The advantage is not always with the new. This book argues that the moral screening we are familiar with makes more sense against the background of its original Christian context. We have learned much about morality over the last two centuries, for example, about how slaves and women have been oppressed by traditional systems previously thought to be morally justified. However, if we remove the moral screening from its original theological context, we stop being able to explain how the good moral life can be accomplished and how the moral life has authority for us. The worldview that retains the context has more explanatory resources and is for that reason to be preferred.

This section has tried to show that community, while it has many benefits, leads to relativism if it is taken as the source of the authority of morality. After distinguishing descriptive relativism from normative relativism, it argued against the second. The main reason to reject normative relativism is that we sometimes need to take a morally critical stance to our culture. Finally, the section discussed how much grounding we can give for preferring one moral screening procedure to another.

Exclusivity

The second danger with overvaluing our community is that it leads to excluding those who do not belong to it. This can happen if we do not see the need to endorse the standards of the community from a position that transcends it. Some philosophers think this kind of endorsement is impossible. They claim that the community gives us our identity, and thus we find or discover our identity rather than making or choosing it; there isn't any position outside the community for us to adopt. Socrates thought of his citizenship in Athens this way, as forming who he was. When he was condemned unjustly to death, he did not think it a realistic possibility for him to escape from prison and live in some other city; to be who he was, he had to stay in Athens. Michael Sandel says about the citizens of a community, "Community describes not just what they have as fellow citizens but also what they are, not a relationship they choose (as in a voluntary association) but an attachment they discover, not merely an attribute but a constituent of their identity." I think it is true that we can "discover" an identity as a citizen of some country, or more broadly as a member of some community. But Sandel's claim relies on an either-or that is not true to experience. Certainly, we can discover an identity, but we also have to choose it.

Amartya Sen gives the example of Mohandas Gandhi, "who had to deliberately decide to give priority to his identification with his fellow-Indians demanding independence from British rule over his identity with his fellow-barristers pursuing English legal justice." His identity had to be chosen as well as discovered. Perhaps it is true that meaning is not something we can construct or invent from scratch for ourselves, because meaning is essentially communal and not private. Because we are, as Aristotle says, social animals, we require that the categories we use to make sense of our lives (like "English" or "professor of philosophy" or "Elvis impersonator") have a social reference larger than we are. But if a person makes the judgment that he should act from such an identity (he should fight for his country or he should teach or he should wear blue suede shoes), he has to endorse this identity, or appropriate it. In that sense, even though he does not make the identity, he makes it *his*.

On ancient Greek racetracks, used for the original Olympic games and described by Homer, the competitors started from a line to which they returned after racing around a turning post. The judges sat on the line to determine who won the race, but the most desired seats for spectators were opposite the turning post; in a chariot race this is where there was the best chance of seeing someone killed as the chariots tried to maneuver close to the post. Applied to the moral life this analogy means that people end up with the same identity conferred on them by their culture. But even so, they must go around the turning post if they are to be morally mature, and this means appropriating the vision of the good life around which that identity is organized. Every identity has to have such a vision if it is going to sustain a person's loyalty through a lifetime. It has to have a way to rank what good things are more important and what good things are less, so that the person living by it can make appropriate choices of what to pursue and what to avoid.

What is the turning post? In this book I have urged a moral screening procedure, which allows the morally responsible appropriation or endorsement of the identity and the vision of the good life we receive from our communities. This screening prevents exclusivity because it gives all human beings the same value whether they belong to our communities or not. Some communities already have this moral reference point of equal value built into the culture which they transmit. But some do not, like Homer's. In those cultures people will be able to appropriate the vision of the good life that they receive from their culture and remain exclusive. Even within cultures like ours, which are familiar with the idea of extending moral relations to all human beings, some philosophers reject it. If we reject it, we will be left with exclusivity.

What I mean by exclusivity is the view that we have moral relations only to the particular people who make up the community that gives us our identity. We could think of this in terms of a woven cloth. The exclusive picture goes like this: "Our identity is to be part of this cloth, and our moral relations are given us by the other threads in the cloth and the patterns they constitute together. The cloth is held together by the weave, which is the caring that the members of the community give to each other. Caring is a rich relation of empathy and identification, which we can only have in relation to comparatively few people. We cannot care for starving children in Zambia when we live in Grand Rapids, because we do not even know who they are." However, this view is objectionable on a number of grounds. Here are three.

First, this exclusivity corrupts the very relations within the community that are supposed to be its home territory. A good illustration is from the smallest community, the family. Families can be dysfunctional where there is abuse of various kinds, emotional or physical or sexual, and not enough caring. But families can also care excessively, or at least disproportionately. The people within special relations like a family have to regard each other not merely as objects of special favor but also as human beings of the same value as any other human beings.

Rosa loves her children, Ned and Lucy. But she has to treat herself as equally valuable with them. This is important for her own sake, but also important for them. If their needs become too pressing for her, she can cease to treat herself as a person with her own dignity. She can forget what is due to herself. There is a baseline of respect for herself; if this line is crossed, she ceases to be able even to give herself to anyone else. She is not, so to speak, there to give, because she has been absorbed, or used up, by the needs of the people she is caring for. This is the danger for Rosa.

The danger for Ned and Lucy is that their mother's unconditional love will give them the wrong impression of themselves. Rosa remembers one especially vivid occasion with Ned. They were at the store shopping for Christmas presents. Ned wanted a certain kind of Lego set, and there was only one such set left on the shelf. Another family was slightly ahead of them. Ned lunged for the Legos, but Rosa held him back. He had expected her to support him and make a scene; but she explained that the other family wanted it as much as he did, and they got there first. A valuable part of this lesson was that it came from Rosa, since Ned knew from experience that he was the apple of his mother's eye. But in this encounter he started to learn to integrate the relations he had to people at home with the relations he had outside. Now that Ned is eighteen, he has learned what respecting a human being is like, with its mixture of valuing what is common and what is unique. He has learned that his mother, too, is a human being. This is a kind of recognition that special relations need if they are going to be morally healthy. To put this most generally, both justice and care are needed in both private and public relations.

A second reason for rejecting exclusivity and insisting on impartial moral screening is that the community identities we discover can become morally vicious. There has been abundant evidence of this on the international scene in the last few decades. A tribal identity is a loyalty to an "us" against a "them." Exclusivity does not see any standards of justice constraining how "we" treat "them." In ancient Greece, Plato records this view in several of the people Socrates encounters. "Justice," says Polemarchus in the *Republic*, "is helping your friends and harming your enemies." Especially if two tribes occupy the same or immediately adjacent regions, all the frustrations that the members of each tribe feel individually can get sluiced, like sewage, into hatred for the other. Leaders use their rhetoric to inflate this hatred for their own advantage, and their followers start to long to defeat or destroy the other tribe as the way to remove their frustrations and get a better life. The result is warfare and, in the extreme, genocide. Nationalism is not the same as patriotism. If I love my country, I should submit it to the same moral scrutiny as any other country because I love it. Nationalism says, "My country right or wrong."

Finally, a third ground for rejecting exclusivity is that if it triumphs, the needs of those who are suffering in the rest of the world will not be met. There are hundreds of thousands of people now who hear about the victims of war or famine or hurricane, and feel they should respond just because it is human beings who are suffering and need their help. If we were to lose this sense of obligation to those outside our communities, many of these needy people would not be helped. It is not merely a matter of being nice but of obligation or obedience. This sense of obligation is an extension of the set of laws in Deuteronomy governing how the community should care for the alien and the stranger (e.g., Deut 15:4–11). The Israelites are in a covenant with God, and within this covenant God expects them to bless others as they themselves have been blessed.

Unlike the Israelites we have been born into a world where we know, through the media, the needs of strangers in all parts of the globe. The problem is that we cannot treat all of them in the way the Good Samaritan in Jesus' parable treated the man who was wounded by the side of the road. We cannot do this because we do not have the resources of time or money or talent. Chapter two discussed this problem in term of the principle of providential proximity. We need a distinction between two groups of obligations. Sometimes we have some freedom of maneuver and some discretion about whom to help and when to help, since we cannot help everyone always. But other times we do not have such discretion; Tom cannot help Ned with his homework if he has to rush Lucy to the hospital with appendicitis. The obligation to help unknown victims of starvation belongs in the first group. Fortunately, our community can extend itself (as described in chapter two) into other parts of the world. When this happens, we can meet the needs of the stranger through that extension. One particular village in Zambia becomes, as it were, our village. But this is no longer exclusivity, because we see this extension as the way providence has given us to meet our universal obligations, which we have to needy human beings as such. Providence is meeting their needs through us.

Community and Providence

Chapter one defined morality as a set of norms for social practice, expressing or supporting values we hold dear and organized by a central directive. But different people develop in different directions in terms of how they internalize these norms and this directive. In one pattern, the individual starts within a web of relationships that give her identity and security, and her moral task is to develop a sense of herself as distinct from that web, and as her own person. In another pattern the person starts with a sense of his distinctness and individuality, and his task is to find a community with which he can merge his identity and cease to be sufficient unto himself. In this section I will use female pronouns for the first pattern and male pronouns for the second because I am drawing on Carol Gilligan's book *In a Different Voice,* in which she develops the idea that these two trajectories are typical of female and male moral development respectively. Chapter three mentioned Jairus and the woman with a hemorrhage, and their stories exemplify these trajectories, though they are also unique. Jesus called Jairus to give up his independence, and he called the woman to stand out from the crowd. But I do not want to tie the distinction tightly to gender differences because there is a valuable point here whether empirical studies confirm the gender differentiation or not. These two patterns of development are both hard to achieve because they both involve a tension between two different ideals of the good human life.

Tom, Rosa's husband, is inclined not to put roots down in the place where he is living but to merely pitch his tent there. He is always open to the thought that he might be called to move. From Rosa's point of view he has itchy feet, and has not learned to "bloom where he is planted." The picture of tenting fits the story of Abraham, who left his people to follow God's call. He "stayed for a time in the land he had been promised, as in a foreign land, living in tents. . . . For he looked forward to the city that has foundations, whose architect and builder is God" (Heb 11:9-10). His loyalty was to the heavenly city, which is eternal, and not to any merely earthly community. Tom, too, is by temperament a resident alien.

This picture is partly attractive and partly repellant. The attractive part is that Tom does not give unconditional commitment to anything like an earthly city that is not unconditionally valuable, and the commitments he does make are authentically his own. Compare this with the person who is a sponge. Oscar Wilde said, "Most people are other people. Their thoughts are someone else's opinion, their lives a mimicry, their passions a quotation." When we see ourselves clearly, it is disconcerting how much of what we think and feel is second-hand. The phrases that form themselves in our heads are usually stock phrases, we find ourselves repeating scenes we have seen on television or at the movies, and our thoughts are what we have been taught to think. I experienced this when I was in India teaching and I tried to learn a meditation technique that involved being conscious of each thought as it entered and left my mind. I was not very successful, partly because I was never physically comfortable with the cross-legged position my body was supposed to adopt while doing the mental exercises. Most of the time I was thinking about how much pain I was in. But I did come to see how utterly derivative my mental contents were. There is something splendid, almost noble, about the person who refuses to attach himself to anything merely second-hand from his community. He insists on first examining each of his commitments and then making them his own, first-hand, if they survive examination.

While there is something attractive about such a person, there is also something repellant. We want to live with people who are loyal to the communities we also belong to and not with people who are merely passing through. The community cannot flourish unless its members have deep roots in it, because its flourishing takes sacrifice and sacrifice takes long-term commitment. Tom's ideal of the examined life, on the other hand, requires detachment. The only way to examine the roots of our ideas and allegiances all the way down is to tear them up to look, and this cannot be done with our commitments unless we detach ourselves from them. But if the roots are going to sustain us, we have to trust them to do much of their work unexamined.

Rosa, on the other hand, likes to put down roots. She likes to belong wholeheartedly to the various communities of her friends, her church, her quartet, and her school, and she knows that this kind of belonging takes time to develop. It takes time because trust takes time to grow and flourish. She finds that she needs a place where others whom she trusts value her and her activities. Her sense of worth comes from her relation to them. It is a real effort for her to distance herself critically from the values of the people around her. In fact it is the relation with them that matters to her fundamentally, not something abstract like "value" at all. She is fully at home in the life of the body of which she is a member, and she finds God in this life. The picture of a body fits what Paul says about our interdependence in Christ. "We who are many form one body, and each member belongs to all the others" (Rom 12:5).

We can put Rosa's perspective in terms of moral specialization. We are each called, in Gerard Manley Hopkins's term, to "selve," to become what we are uniquely fitted to be. But this best kind of life for each of us is best only because other people have different kinds of life that are best for each of them. This is what I mean by moral specialization. We make up *together* the best life for all of us. If we think of the community as a body, we are all different parts of it, and the life of the body requires all those parts to function effectively. The idea here is that people are most useful to others when they are most fully themselves. (This is true even though, as we said in chapter six about Tom's capacity to concentrate on his reading, there are good and bad ways for a person to use who he is.) This specialization only works if each of us knows what the others are good at, and what they can be relied upon to do well. This kind of trust takes a long time to grow.

There is something attractive about this kind of belonging, but also something repellant. If we overemphasize the organic metaphor of being part of a body, we will not give the right kind of freedom to each of its parts. The ancient world was different from ours in the degree to which people identified themselves with their nation. By contrast there is something valuable in the responsibility of each person to respond in his or her own heart to the call of God, not simply through membership in the body. This is true not merely of our relation to God but also to each other. Our sense of worth should not be so dependent on our status in the community. We should not be wrapped so firmly in the cocoon.

We need a way to hold these two different ideals of the good human life together and to integrate them into a unified life. Probably the specific way in which they are integrated will be a matter of moral specialization, different for different people. But one belief that would tie them together fruitfully is the belief that the community we belong to is itself providential. Believing this is risky because we do not always fit the places where we are and sometimes it seems right to move. I write here as an emigrant. But a picture of providence that helps resolve this difficulty is the picture of Rosa's classroom outlined in chapter eight.

Rosa divides her class into cooperative learning groups. She knows the personalities and skills of all her students, and she sorts them into groups accordingly. Some of them are quicker on the uptake, some of them have more developed social skills, and some of them are just plain difficult (though she insists she loves all of them the same). She has a flexible curriculum so that she can assign tasks to each group that fit it, and within each group tasks will also get split up differently. But the grouping is not immutable. Because Rosa also has a direct relation to each student, not merely a relation through the group, she can see when things are not going well, and she can reassign a student to a different group. Sometimes a student will initiate the change, and sometimes Rosa will do it herself. In either case, if she does it right, the result will be better learning for everybody.

If we see providence guiding us to a community as a gift, in the way the learning groups are Rosa's gift to her students, we can overcome at least in theory the difficulties with both Tom's picture and Rosa's. The problem with Tom's picture is that he seems too detached. But if he believes that God has put him in a community, then his very faith-ideal requires him to be communally attached. It is as though the heavenly city requires him to find an earthly one in which to grow and flourish, so that he cannot be faithful to the first without being loyal to the second. This would be what Gilligan calls the male pattern of reaching moral maturity: he develops into community.

The problem with Rosa's picture is that she seems too caught up in her different communities. But if the community is really where she goes to find God, then her very loyalty to the group requires her to be faithful beyond the group to the God who has put her there. She cannot be loyal to the first without being faithful to the second. This would be what Gilligan calls the female pattern of moral development: she develops into personal integrity. In both cases it is the connection of the community with providence that allows the person to develop into moral maturity, which combines both belonging and a proper sense of self. We need to be attached to something beyond the community if we are going to attach ourselves to the community in the right way.

This chapter has argued that community is not the source of the authority of morality. To regard it as such a source is to make it into what Christianity calls an idol. The chapter traced the dangers of relativism and exclusivity that come from this kind of idolatry. Finally, it suggested that community can be the source of great good if we see that it is itself a gift. As argued in the previous three chapters, the various proposed sources of authority can have the value they should when located in the context of theological belief. The present chapter has not argued that this is the only context in which this could happen in the case of community. However, any other context will need to have the same feature as theological belief—that it can confer value on community membership from outside the community.

10

Autonomy

The last four chapters have proposed that moral perception, human nature, human reason and community are not enough to answer the question "Why should I be moral?" Belief that morality is God's call to us provides in each case a context in which we can see the proper value of these good things. Belief in God explains how moral value comes from outside us, how we are fulfilled by living morally, how a moral life has significance and how we get from morality a proper sense of belonging.

This final chapter deals with our response to God's call and our freedom in relation to that response. The challenge is to understand the proper limits of human autonomy. The chapter explores a good way to understand autonomy—as appropriation. It then gives a description of how this kind of freedom relates to a firm moral character. The chapter ends by looking at the restlessness which still affects our moral life on earth.

The term *autonomy* combines two Greek words: *autos,* which means "self," and *nomos,* which means "law." The basic idea, as Immanuel Kant expressed it, is that we ourselves have to make moral law. There is a helpful way of understanding this, which is Kant's own way, and an unhelpful way, which has been typical of many of Kant's successors. These successors have often (mistakenly, I think) read their view back into Kant. (But I am not writing a book about Kant, so I will not try to defend this claim.)

The helpful way to think of autonomy is to think of it as appropriation, as making the moral law our own. This implies that we do not invent or create the moral law, but we make it ours by bringing our wills in line with it. Kant says that we should recognize our duties as God's commands and that we should believe that God exists and gives us these commands, even though God is beyond the limits of human understanding.

The unhelpful way puts the challenge to believers in God like this: "If we are going to be autonomous, to make moral law ourselves, we have to be independent of any external authority, whether that is external human authority or the external authority of God. Our freedom is for an eighth day of creation, in which we create ourselves, no longer under the tutelage of a deity from on high. We are no longer children but adults. Religion, as a source of moral authority, may have been necessary before universal education and the birth of modern science. But we are now in a position to emancipate ourselves from superstitious fears and traditions and find our own path toward a better life for all humankind."

This second view of autonomy belongs together with a certain view of our intellectual history. J. B. Schneewind puts it this way, "As God's supervision and activity lessen, man's responsibility increases." He constructs an ironic picture of something he calls "the Divine Corporation," which is rather like the corporation in which the cartoon character Dilbert finds himself employed. In the Divine Corporation ordinary employees understand very little about each other's jobs or the purposes of the company as a whole. They are paid for carrying out their duties strictly, "looking neither to left nor to right." If they foul up their little tasks, someone else will clear up the mess and they do not feel responsible for the remedy themselves. This, says Schneewind, is the traditional Christian picture of the kingdom of God, with God as the head of the firm. Progress toward autonomy, he thinks, occurs in the history of ethics as these conditions weaken. We come to see that we are responsible for promoting human happiness and we do this by cooperating with each other, understanding each other's contributions and repairing our omissions when we can.

Schneewind then traces this progress in the history of European moral philosophy from the Middle Ages up to Immanuel Kant in the eighteenth century. I think he misreads Kant, but I do not want to deny that moral philosophers after Kant have taken some of the steps Schneewind describes. The question whether this was *progress*, however, still needs to be settled. In the language of chapter one, this is a normative question, not merely a descriptive one. In other words the changes were only progress if they were changes for the better. Changes in philosophical fashion can be a mixture of progress and regress. That, at least, is what I am going to suggest has happened with our changing understanding of human freedom.

On the unhelpful view of autonomy, morally successful human lives will be ones that reach their own human goals, defined in their own human terms and using their own human resources. We will have no need to appeal to divine assistance to help us reach a goal too high for us by our own resources. The doctrines described in chapter three will be entirely unnecessary. But whether this view is progress or not depends on whether there is or isn't a God who makes the kind of call discussed in this book and offers us the resources to follow it. If there is such a God, such a call and such assistance, and if a person senses this but refuses to acknowledge it, then this person, and not the believer in God, is being childish.

Rosa's daughter Lucy is learning the piano. Her teacher has written marks above the notes on Lucy's new piece to indicate which fingers she should use to make the piece more expressive and easier to play; however, Lucy refuses to learn the fingering because she does not see the point. She insists on setting her own goals, defining them in her own terms and using her own resources. In a word, she insists on autonomy. The result is that she never plays the piece as well as she could. She always stumbles over certain passages; and the more she practices them, the more the poor way of playing them gets programmed into her fingers so that it gets harder and harder to change it. Consequently, neither Lucy nor anyone else gets the pleasure they could from her playing the piece, and in the end she gives it up. From her teacher's point of view this is not autonomy but a sad waste of her abilities.

Our situation with God is different because unlike the piano student with her teacher we do not literally see God. This is not because God is defective but because the divine nature is spirit. The twentieth-century philosopher Bertrand Russell, who did not believe in God, imagined himself after his death facing the final judgment and complaining to God that God had not given him enough evidence. But if the nonbeliever has a sense of this kind of call, higher than he can reach by his own devices, and if he has a sense of the possibility of this kind of assistance, the key will be what he does with that sense of possibility. Kierkegaard calls this "the dizziness of freedom." There is evidence from Russell's life that he did feel something like this periodically and rejected it as an illusion. From the believer's point of view, the decisive evidence that assistance is available comes only when a person starts to follow the call. Unfortunately we do not get this kind of security in advance. We need, therefore, what chapter four calls "moral faith," the faith that despite the contrary evidence we can be transformed and that we can be happy without compromising the attempt to be morally good.

Rosa's son Ned, when he was younger, once climbed a tree, and when he started to descend and looked down at the ground, he lost his confidence and found that he could not trust himself to let go of the branch he was holding onto. He panicked for a moment. He could have been stuck there until the fire brigade arrived with a ladder. In fact, however, he let himself swing down to the branch below and behold it supported him. In order to get free from his temporary paralysis, Ned needed not more evidence, but more courage—a virtue primarily of the will rather than the intellect.

Appropriation

If we do not have complete evidence in advance that following God's call will lead us to a morally successful life, how do we know that the call is not merely arbitrary? We can get trapped here by a false dilemma. We might think that we have to choose between the following two pictures. In one picture the moral screening is the guide to whether an act is right, and we put everything through this screening, including what we initially take to be a call from God. The problem is that this seems to make ourselves and our screening the final authority, rather than God. In the other picture we should sometimes follow what we initially take to be God's call even if it doesn't pass the screening test. But then we could be led to do all sorts of horrendous things, given the tricks that our disordered imaginations can play on us (or, for that matter, the tricks of malevolent demons).

Ned is at college and wakes up in the middle of the night with the idea that God is telling him to kill his roommate. He tells himself that this couldn't be God, since God doesn't tell people to do that sort of thing. But then he remembers the story of Abraham and Isaac. It is true that Abraham did not actually have to kill his son, because God provided a ram for the sacrifice at the last minute; however, Abraham was ready to kill, and according to the story, God did give him that command. Ned knows the interpretation that Abraham believed God would bring Isaac back to life, since God had promised offspring through Isaac as numerous as the grains of sand on the seashore and the stars in the sky. Does this mean, Ned wonders, that he should believe that God will bring his roommate back to life? Or would this simply be crazy? He decides that in this case it was just a weird dream, and he prays about it and then goes back to fitful sleep.

The mistake here is to think that we have to choose between the authority of moral screening and the authority of God's call. The truth is that for a believer this is a complex and rich mixture. Robert Adams describes the mixture this way: "[The believer] regards his moral principles as given him by God and adheres to them partly out of love or loyalty to God, but he also prizes them for their own sakes, so that they are the principles he *would* give himself if he were giving himself a moral law. In so far as he is right, [he] acts morally because he loves God, but also because he loves what God loves." We and God both intend that we should reach our final destination, which is being co-lovers with God. We do not know much about what this final destination is like. Our ancestors who are there (if they are) have not come back to tell us. But the three features of the organizing directive described in chapter one reflect features of that state. We will, in that state, see the whole of creation more nearly than we do now and love it as a whole. We will see Christ in each other more clearly and so value each one through our love of Christ, and we will be free of the disproportionate love for the self that we have on earth. We will see more clearly our own individual essences (being given the white stone with our name) and the uniqueness of others. These ways in which we will then love are ways in which we imitate God's love for us, having been "renewed in the knowledge in the image of [our] Creator" (Col 3:10 NIV). God sees the whole, sees us in Christ and sees our uniqueness. When we love each other in these ways we are sharing an end with God.

The moral norms like the prohibitions on murder and lying are a route to this end and not a deduction from human nature. God can therefore give a human being some other route to this end and perhaps with Abraham this is what God did. But when we follow the route God has given us, we are doing so both because God has given it to us and because it is a route to the end which we share with God.

Suppose we grant that God did command Abraham to kill his innocent son. Does this mean we should worry about whether God will tell us to do the same kind of thing? We should acknowledge that God sometimes calls us to do things when we do not yet understand how they are consistent with our final destination. But this is not the same as telling us to do something that contradicts the route we have been given. God is free to do even this, and in the case of the laws about sacrifice and diet in the Hebrew Scriptures, the early Christians claimed that God did so. But in the case of the moral law, we have been given evidence of the blessing for us and others that follows obedience. Though we sometimes have to obey without understanding, it does not follow that we are free to go around killing innocent people. We have seen how morality fits human nature and how when we keep it we flourish and when we break it we deteriorate. Abraham had not yet been given the revelation either of the route or of the blessing (though we might argue that some knowledge of the route is given to every human being); we have been given both. Our attitude should therefore be that of the Lord's prayer, "Lead us not into temptation." This is not the odd prayer that God will not tempt us. Rather, we are praying that God will not lead us into a time of trial, like the testing of Abraham.

Rosa's husband, Tom, receives an invitation to apply for a job, and he hears in this the call to end his present employment, leave his and Rosa's extended family and move to a school affiliated with a denomination he has never heard of in a distant city where they know nobody at all. But he and Rosa have moral faith, and so this call does not seem arbitrary to them, even though they do not understand how it will lead to blessing for their family and their work. They have previously experienced blessing following this kind of obedience, when they understood afterward but not beforehand why God was telling them to do something. They also know that they might be wrong about this call; it might not be anything more than Tom's characteristically itchy feet. He tends to think about moving whenever he hears the geese crying overhead in the late fall. They know that they need to check this as best they can, using not only their own moral screening but also the advice of people they trust, the Scriptures and the interpretation of the Scriptures in their tradition.

There is a question here that I will discuss only briefly, though it deserves a whole chapter (or a whole book). Are we ever put in a situation in which it is necessary to break one of the moral norms? A Dutch householder during the Second World War is hiding a Jew in his attic and is asked by a Nazi officer whether he has any Jews in his house. Should he lie to save the man's life? On the view presented in chapter one, the organizing directive does not replace the moral norms but organizes them. We cannot, therefore, simply override the norm of truthfulness in the name of love or compassion. Lying to a Nazi is not loving him, though it may be loving the Jew hidden in the attic. Perhaps in this tragic situation there is no way to love both of them, and this means there is no way for the moral screening to completely approve any action. Nonetheless, lying does seem less bad than betraying the life. We need a category of "least bad" which is not the same as "morally permitted" or "right." Sometimes we may have to do what is least bad, even though it is not a fully loving thing to do.

If Tom and Rosa take the call to move, they are being obedient, but they are also being autonomous according to the first view of autonomy distinguished earlier. They are making what they believe to be God's call, their own will. They are autonomous because they are appropriating the call. The verb *appropriate* comes from two Latin words: *ad*, meaning "(bringing) to," and *proprium*, meaning "one's own." Tom and Rosa are bringing this call into their own wills, or bringing their wills into line with the call. They are trying to repeat in their wills God's will for their willing. But we can repeat another person's will with many different degrees of clarity and fullness.

Rosa is afraid that Ned is about to start sleeping with his girlfriend. There are many different possible frames of mind in which Ned could comply with his mother's wishes. He might do what she wants because he loves her and does not want to make her unhappy, but without understanding or sharing her vision of the spiritual union properly surrounding sexual intercourse. Or he might not love her but might just dislike the antagonism that would be caused by disappointing her. In fact, in Ned's case he does share some of his mother's views, though not all of them. He does not have her certainty about this issue, and he does not feel like confronting his many friends and acquaintances who hold different views. He also thinks the biblical texts are less black and white than his mother does. His girlfriend has the same kind of uncertainty that he does; if she really wanted to have sex right away, perhaps he would go along with her. Moreover, Ned is not completely clear about his mother's position. She talked to him about her fears, but she also stressed her respect for his judgment and his greater knowledge about his own life. All this left him wondering whether she was signaling a willingness to change her mind.

We can share the ends of other people more or less closely, and the same is true in our relation to God. Perhaps we can never have complete clarity or full comprehension about the purposes we share with God and the route God has given us. We can approximate this to various degrees, depending on how well we know God and how well we know ourselves. But we have only the limited access to God's will that God has given us. We therefore have to contribute our own thinking, working out what is best, always keeping in mind the dangers of self-deception and remembering the guidelines we have been given.

Firmness

Duns Scotus describes two types of freedom. We can understand the first by comparing a human with an armadillo, which looks for an ant to eat and then consumes it. The armadillo does not really have freedom, even though it has an internal source of motion. We would be the same way, Scotus says, if we had only the motivation toward happiness (though our pursuit of happiness would be more complicated than the armadillo's). As described in chapter four, however, he thinks we also have the motivation toward what is good in itself, independent of our happiness, and this takes us beyond our natural goal of happiness. Because we have both types of motivation, the question arises for us how we are going to rank them. And because we can ask this question, we reach the first type of freedom. We have the possibility of going in both directions, depending on what we will, either ranking first what is good in itself or our happiness.

We can also have a second type of freedom beyond this one, which Scotus calls "firmness." This is the kind of freedom God has. If we ask the question, Can God sin? we run into problems either way. If we say no, we are apparently limiting God's omnipotence and freedom. Surely God can do everything. But if we say yes, we are saying God can be inconsistent with the divine nature. Scotus suggests that God's freedom is beyond the possibility of going in both directions. Unlike God, we get to firmness through freedom of the first sort. The motivation toward what is good in itself is a move beyond nature and firmness is a further move in the same direction. Firmness is where our love of the good has become so large a part of us through our constant choosing that there is no room left for serious defection. In heaven we will not be able to sin, but that is not because we will have less freedom than we do on earth but because we will have more. We do not become God, but we become like God in this respect as we become co-lovers with God.

What does this mean for our freedom on earth? We can hope to move in the direction of less uncertainty and more firmness. Chapters one and three described sanctification as the movement toward a state in which attraction and constraint come together. If we reach that state, what we want to do will fit gracefully with what we ought to do. It will not be necessary to check so frequently whether our inclination fits with our duty. This is not the same as merely getting comfortable, which can just be the product of getting older. People can get more comfortable with their overall commitments in the way they get used to their old shoes. The comfort may simply be moral laziness if they stop attending to the gap between their talk and their walk. How do we tell the difference between firmness and this kind of comfortableness?

In the case of life commitments, there are some constraints we can think of as sanctions. We can control whether we activate the starting conditions; but once we have done that, the consequences will follow, as physical pain follows overuse or underuse of the muscles, unless we do something else to counteract them. Human nature and individual nature are not infinitely malleable. If we choose not to follow a route that fits those natures, we are likely to start malfunctioning in various ways, both outside and inside. To some extent we can see these effects in ourselves and in other people. If we do not see them, that is some confirmation that we and they are still growing forward.

Chapter seven gave the example of truthfulness. If we stop sincerely valuing truth, there are consequences for our relation to the *outside* (quasi-magnetic) center which holds together the attractions which pull us. Truthfulness is necessary to keep open our receptivity to those signals. It often takes hard work to attend to them, and we are tempted to allow a crust to form around ourselves that prevents unfamiliar signals from getting through. When we see vivid examples of people with our own failings, we need to be truthful as we go through the process of acknowledgment and repentance in the *inside* center (the will). We have a tendency to deceive ourselves, so that when we are presented with some unflattering picture of ourselves, we convince ourselves that it does not show us as we really are. We deteriorate morally when we stop being able to hear or to approve messages calling us to change. So here is a sign: If we stop hearing the insistent call to change, we are getting too comfortable.

This example of truthfulness is just one case where failure in one part of the call leads to more general deterioration. Another case is a disordered relation to parents, which ends up distorting a person's vision of large tracts of her life through various complicated tricks of her psychology. Similarly, coveting a neighbor's property leads us to stop seeing his goodness and to exaggerate his defects. We start to see him as someone who doesn't deserve to have those things. But then we have to start deceiving ourselves about whether we deserve to have ours. Claiming we have earned our blessings is another sign of moral decay. There are also consequences related to our unique natures. We sometimes hear the call and refuse to align our will. There will be consequences for our lives and the lives of people we care about. We will feel a gradual sense of separation from the source of the call and an attendant isolation. Life does not allow us to stay neutral. We are always moving forward or backward, even if we try not to change, because the call is always there and we are always moving toward or away from it.

Moving toward more firmness, therefore, is not merely getting more comfortable with our commitments, as though they were old shoes. We can distinguish patterns of moral maturation and decay, and these are the framework within which our autonomy operates. They are patterns that give our lives a good shape to grow into. A person gets more solid, or firm, as he "becomes what he is." Chapter seven discussed this paradoxical phrase. The idea is that our nature, both human and unique, gives us a direction and we fulfill that nature by following that direction. Firmness, or solidity, is saying with Luther, "Here I stand; I cannot do otherwise."

Restlessness

Firmness is not the whole story about maturation. Why did God not make us firm right away? Wouldn't we have been better off if we had been given a stronger natural tendency to resist evil (perhaps strong enough to defeat Satan's temptation in the Garden)? George Herbert's poem "The Pulley" gives us the beginning of an answer.

> When God at first made man,
> Having a glass of blessings standing by,
> "Let us," said he, "pour on him all we can:
> Let the world's riches, which dispersed lie,
>   Contract into a span."
>   So strength first made a way;
> Then beauty flowed, then wisdom, honour, pleasure;
> When almost all was out, God made a stay,
> Perceiving that, alone of all his treasure,
>   Rest in the bottom lay.
>   "For if I should," said he,
> "Bestow this jewel also on my creature,
> He would adore my gifts instead of me,
> And rest in nature, not the God of Nature:
>   So both should losers be.
>   "Yet let him keep the rest,
> But keep them with repining restlessness;
> Let him be rich and weary, that at least,
> If goodness lead him not, yet weariness
>   May toss him to my breast."

In this poem Herbert inverts the traditional story of Pandora's box. In one version of the Greek myth, Epimetheus (who is human) opens the box and all the blessings of the gods fly out of it except for hope, which he retains. The result is that we humans do not have those other blessings, but at least we can hope for them. Herbert's story goes the other way round. God is imagined as an alchemist making a new substance from a glass full of precious elements. This new substance is going to be an example in miniature of everything that is best in the world. The result is that we humans have all these blessings (strength, beauty, wisdom, honour, pleasure) except for the one that God retains: rest.

Why does God keep it back? Because if God gives it to us, we will start to worship the blessings and not God, and we will make an idol out of nature. Then, God says in the poem, both we and God will lose. Here is the self-limitation I described at the end of chapter five. God, by creating us and loving us, becomes vulnerable to our choices. Herbert then offers us a pun, which is not merely a pun. God says in the poem, "Let him keep the rest, but keep them with repining [dissatisfied] restlessness" (the word *restlessness* drags the meter, so that we can feel the uneasiness). This is a pun (the two meanings of rest come from quite different roots, old German and Latin) but not merely a pun (because there is a kind of deficient rest available in the rest of the blessings). Is God being cruel in condemning us to weariness? Herbert here reminds us of Augustine, who prayed to God, at the beginning of the *Confessions,* "You have made us for yourself and our heart is restless until it rests in you." A kind of lack in us prevents us resting too soon, and this lack ends up tossing us to God like a piece of flotsam tossed onto the shore in a storm. The restlessness is part of the route that a loving God prescribes to us.

What is this restlessness? We feel something present as well as something absent. Ecclesiastes 3:11 says that God put eternity into our hearts but in such a way that we cannot discover the whole course of what God has done from the beginning to the end. We have here a conviction about what is possible for us as well as a sense of dissatisfaction because of what is not possible. This combination affects both the intellect as we try to understand and the will as we try to love. Kant describes the dissatisfaction of the intellect. in the first sentence of the *Critique of Pure Reason,* saying that human reason has the peculiar fate of being given by its own nature the burden of asking questions which, because of the very same nature, it is unable to answer. We have the conviction that there is a reality beyond our understanding, beckoning to us but eluding our grasp. This is the restlessness of the understanding. We are stuck with it, and it is in the end a gift. We learn the limits of our understanding by pushing against them, and we learn how to believe things that we do not yet understand.

We are also given the aspiration to a kind of love that we find ourselves unable to live up to by our own resources. Chapter one said that morality consists of various norms, like the requirement to keep our promises, but also a directive which organizes them. The Christian background to this directive is the command to love our neighbor as ourselves. But loving each other in this way turns out to be a demand too high for us by our own devices. Here is the dissatisfaction of the will. God made us free by giving us this tension—a tension between our defective loving and the conviction that we are joined by adoption to Christ's love. This adoption was one topic of chapter three. We feel the gap between our feeble attempts and the love that is already complete and invites us to come closer. This tension can bring us in the end to a more perfect union with God if we rely on God's assistance to resolve it. We have only to avoid resting too soon—resting in nature, not the God of nature. If we are attentive to it, restlessness will prevent us from doing this. It will take us beyond the goodness of the gifts to the goodness of the giver.

What, then, is the relation between morality and God? A good word to end with is covenant. Covenants differ in various ways from contracts. Consider a covenant like marriage. The partners are taking on commitments beyond what they can foresee, they do not know just what they are covenanting to do, and the needs and gifts of the partners can change without the covenant dissolving. Shakespeare relies on this conception in the sonnet we discussed in chapter eight: "Love is not love which alters when it alteration finds." The believer is in a covenant with God that involves (as in a marriage) having the common destination of a union between them. Part of this covenant, for example the second group of the Ten Commandments, covers human relations with other humans. This is summed up in the command "Love your neighbor as your self," which includes but also goes beyond the earlier norms. If we were merely in a contract with God, our inability to carry out our part would dissolve the relation. But because we are in a covenant, God gives us the assistance we need when we ask for it.

In this book I have tried to describe what this assistance is like. The first part discussed the doctrines of atonement, justification, sanctification and providence. The second part described what difference God's initiative in the covenant makes to our desires for transcendence, fulfillment, significance and belonging. When we put all this together we have an ethics that is both like and unlike an ethics which removes the context of the covenant. The moral demand without God is in many ways the same. We still have to keep our promises, we have to be grateful to our benefactors, and above all these we have to care about the whole to which we belong and respect the equality and uniqueness of persons. But now there are problems both on the side of our capacity to comply and on the side of the authority of the demand. On the capacity side, when we lose the context of the covenant, it is not clear that we *can* live that way. We no longer have the resources of Christ's life in us, or of his church, or his forgiveness. On the demand side, what is the source of the demand's authority? Why *should* we live that way? Without answers to these questions, we face the threat of incoherence, and the

moral life becomes unlike what it was in its initial context. It
becomes desperate, or grim, or compromised. I have described some
of the results. We pretend to ourselves that we are better than we
actually are, or that the moral demand is just an ideal and not something to which we are actually accountable. Or we fill the gap with
various attractions, or self-realization schemes, or rational systems, or
communal attachments, none of which (if I have made my case) succeed by themselves in the task we give them.

The appropriate response to God's grace within the covenant
might seem to be one of grateful subservience. And there is much
language in Scripture about serving and obeying God. But our destination is not, in fact, to be merely servants, but to be co-lovers or
friends. The character of our final relation with God will not be one
of constraint or even attraction as to a magnet. It will not be demand
or even call. It is hard to imagine what it will be like. But George
Herbert, in the final and perhaps the greatest poem of his collection,
gives us a picture of what the transition will be like. He imagines
Christ as Love, who bids him welcome (now at the Eucharist and
finally at the heavenly banquet), and he describes the dialogue
between them, which follows the order of the Anglican Communion
service. Herbert pictures himself hesitating in his guilt and repentance:

> But quick-eyed Love, observing me grow slack
>   From my first entrance in,
> Drew nearer to me, sweetly questioning
>   If I lacked anything.
> "A guest," I answered, "worthy to be here"
>   Love said, "You shall be he."

Here Love shows Herbert that he is justified, that he is already
worthy though he has not yet experienced his worthiness. Herbert
pulls back again; he cannot look on Love. But Love says that he has

made the eyes for Herbert to look, and he has borne the blame for
Herbert's sin. Herbert's self-importance is finally shamed into desist-
ing. He offers to serve at the meal. But Love refuses even this offer.

> "You must sit down," says Love, "and taste my meat."
> So I did sit and eat.

The restlessness ends with rest. We are told that we will then know
even as we are known (1 Cor 13:12). I think it is true also that we
will then love even as we are loved. There will no longer be the qual-
itative gap between the loving we want to do and the loving we are
doing, though there may still be growth in loving even then. Much
of morality as we are familiar with it will fade away. It was always just
a skin that we could outgrow. There will no longer be norms to stop
us from murdering or lying or coveting, and there will be no directive to organize these norms. There will be no constraint and no
attraction from a distant source. What should we think, though,
about those three parts of the picture that we started with: the
wholeness of creation, or its integrity, the high value of people in this
creation and their equal value, and the uniqueness of all persons? I
suppose the importance of these might fade away too. We do not
know much about how we will love what is not God, though we
know that we will be co-lovers with God. However, I am convinced
that we will still value something like the integrity of creation and
the equality and uniqueness of the persons God has made and that
valuing them will be part of the love that is our final destination.

Bibliography

[Books are listed in the order of their appearance in each chapter.]

Introduction
John E. Hare. *The Moral Gap*. Oxford: Clarendon Press, 1996.

John E. Hare. *God's Call*. Grand Rapids, Mich.: Eerdmans, 2001.

Chapter 1: Morality
Ogden Nash. "Kind of an Ode to Duty." In *I'm a Stranger Here Myself*. London: Little, Brown, 1959.

John E. Hare and Carey B. Joynt. *Ethics and International Affairs*. London: Macmillan, 1981

Chapter 2: The Moral Gap Without God
Henry Bedinger Mitchell, ed. *Talks on Religion*. New York: Longmans, Green, 1908.

Albert Shaw. *Municipal Government in Great Britain*. 1895. Quoted in Ebenezer Howard, *Garden Cities of To-Morrow*. London: Faber & Faber, 1945.

M. S. Dworkin. *Dewey on Education*. New York: Bureau of Publications, Teachers' College, Columbia University, 1959.

"A Humanist Manifesto," *The New Humanist* 6, no. 3 (1933).

T. K. Stanton. "Liberal Arts. Experiential Learning and Public Service: Necessary Ingredients for Socially Responsible Undergraduate Education," in *Combining Service and Learning*. Edited by J. C. Kendall. Vol. 1. Raleigh, N.C.: National Society for Internships and Experiential Education, 1990.

James Kunstler. "Where Evil Dwells," paper presented at Congress for the New Urbanism, Milwaukee, Wisconsin, 1999.

Immanuel Kant. *The Metaphysics of Morals*. Translated by Mary Gregor. Cambridge:

Cambridge University Press, 1991.

J. S. Mill. *Utilitarianism*. London: Collins, 1962.

Shelley Kagan. *The Limits of Morality*. New York: Oxford University Press, 1989.

John Dewey. *The Later Works*. Edited by Jo Ann Boydston, Carbondale: Southern Illinois University Press, 1961-1990.

Plato. *Meno*. In *The Collected Dialogues of Plato*. Princeton, N.J.: Princeton University Press, 1961.

Nel Noddings. *Caring*. Berkeley: University of California Press, 1984.

Larry Arnhart. *Darwinian Natural Right*. Albany: State University of New York Press, 1998.

Michael Ruse. *Can a Darwinian Be a Christian?* New York: Cambridge University Press, 2001.

R. H. Frank, T. Gilovich and D. Regan. "Does Studying Economics Inhibit Cooperation?" *Journal of Economic Perspectives* 7 (1993).

James Griffin. *Well-Being*. Oxford: Clarendon Press, 1986.

Philip Hefner. *The Human Factor*. Minneapolis: Fortress, 1993.

Chapter 3: God's Assistance

John Donne. "Ecstasy." In *The Norton Anthology of Poetry*. New York: Norton, 1996.

Gerard Manley Hopkins. "As Kingfishers Catch Fire" and "The Windhover." In *The Norton Anthology of Poetry*. New York: Norton, 1996.

Chapter 4: Providence

Bernard Williams. *Shame and Necessity*. Berkeley: Univerisity of California Press, 1994.

A. E. Housman. "Terence, This Is Stupid Stuff." In *The Norton Anthology of Poetry*. New York: Norton, 1996.

Nicholas Wolterstorff. *Lament for a Son*. Grand Rapids, Mich: Eerdamns, 1987.

C. S. Lewis. *A Grief Observed*. San Francisco: Harper, 1994.

Joni Earickson Tada and Steve Estes. *A Step Further*. Grand Rapids, Mich.: Zondervan, 1978.

Chapter 5: The Authority of Morality

Immanuel Kant. *Religion Within the Limits of Reason Alone*. Translated by Theodore M. Greene and Hoyt H. Hudson. New York: Harper & Row, 1960.

Chapter 6: Goodness

Plato. *Ion*. In *The Collected Dialogues of Plato*. Princeton, N.J.: Princeton University Press, 1961.

Chapter 7: Human Nature

J. Z. Young. *An Introduction to the Study of Man.* Oxford: Clarendon Press, 1971.

Aristotle. *Nicomachean Ethics.* Translated by Terence Irwin. Indianapolis: Hackett, 1999.

Chapter 8: Reason

Thomas Carson. *Value and the Good Life.* South Bend, Ind.: University of Notre Dame Press, 2000.

J. David Velleman. "Brandt's Definition of 'Good,' " *Philosophical Review* 97 (1988).

Søren Kierkegaard. *Either/Or.* Edited and translated by Howard and Edna Hong. Princeton, N.J.: Princeton University Press, 1987.

James D. Bratt, ed. *Abraham Kuyper: A Centennial Reader.* Grand Rapids, Mich.: Eerdmans, 1998.

Shakespeare. "Sonnet 116." In *The Norton Anthology of Poetry.* New York: Norton, 1996.

Immanuel Kant. *Critique of Pure Reason.* Translated by Norman Kemp Smith. New York: St. Martin's, 1965.

Chapter 9: Community

Theognis, quoted in J. B. Bury. *History of Greece.* London: Macmillan, 1963.

Amartya Sen, "Other People," *The New Republic,* December 18, 2000.

Plato. *Republic.* In *The Collected Dialogues of Plato.* Princeton, N.J.: Princeton University Press, 1961.

Carol Gilligan. *In a Different Voice.* Cambridge, Mass.: Harvard University Press, 1993.

Chapter 10: Autonomy

J. B. Schneewind. "The Divine Corporation and the History of Ethics." In *Philosophy and History.* Edited by Richard Rorty, J. B. Schneewind and Quentin Skinner. Cambridge: Cambridge University Press, 1984.

Robert M. Adams. "Autonomy and Theological Ethics." In *The Virtue of Faith.* Oxford: Oxford University Press, 1987.

Allan Wolter, ed. and trans. *Duns Scotus on the Will and Morality.* Washington, D.C.: Catholic University of America Press, 1997.

George Herbert. "The Pulley" and "Love (III)." In *The Norton Anthology of Poetry.* New York: Norton, 1996.

Augustine. *Confessions.* Translated by Henry Chadwick. Oxford: Oxford University Press, 1991.

Index

Names and Subjects

Scripture